REFLECTIONS
DEVELOPING PROFICIENCY IN ENGLISH

Instructor's Guide

Patricia Munro Conway
Dyanne Rivers

Pippin Publishing Limited

Copyright © 1995 by Pippin Publishing Limited
481 University Avenue
Toronto, Ontario
M5G 2E9

All rights reserved. No part of this publication may be reproduced or transmitted in any form or by any means, electronic, mechanical or otherwise, including photocopying and recording, or stored in any retrieval system without permission in writing from the publisher.

Designed by John Zehethofer
Printed and bound by Canadian Printco Limited

Canadian Cataloguing in Publication Data

Munro Conway, Patricia
  Reflections: developing proficiency in English.
Instructor's Guide

Supplement to: Munro-Conway, Patricia. Reflections: developing proficiency in English
ISBN 0-88751-071-X

1. English language - Rhetoric - Study and teaching.
2. English language - Problems, exercises, etc. 3. Role playing - Study and teaching. 4. English language - Study and teaching as a second language.*
I. Rivers, Dyanne. II. Title.

PE1408.M852 1995   808'.0427   C95-931587-X

ISBN 0-88751-071-X

10 9 8 7 6 5 4 3 2 1

Contents

Introduction 5

PART 1 Readings and Reading Activities

Verb Tenses at a Glance 16
  1 A Traveller's Tale 18
  2 A Visitor 23
  3 Going for the Gold 27
  4 The Day It Rained Forever 31
  5 Human Rights and Human Responsibilities 35
  6 The Shape of the Law 39
  7 The Wages of Sin 43
  8 The Avalon Notes *and* Ten Years with the Same Dog 48
  9 My Private Solitude 53
10 The Stepmother 56
11 THE ESSAY
    Family Silliness, Domestic Clowning 60
    On Hope and Suicide 62
12 POETRY
    The Road Not Taken 67
    Aftermath 68
    The Shark 70
    To My Son 71
    from *Tao Teh Ching* 72
    Ynne Auncient Daeyes 75
13 DRAMA
    from *Bethune* 76

PART 2 Oral Activities

14 Scenarios from Everyday Life *80*
15 Short-Term Gain—Long-Term Pain? *81*
16 Inheritance *83*
17 Desperately Seeking… *84*
18 Whose Needs Come First? *85*
19 Work and the Family *86*
20 The Continuing Story of… *87*
21 A Living Will *88*
22 Best Interests of the Child *89*
23 The Best Candidate *90*
24 Who's at Fault? *91*
25 Whodunit? *92*

Introduction

Like all learners, English as a second language students flourish in a supportive environment that is sensitive to their individual circumstances. Instructors play a key role in creating this environment, guiding and challenging students as they develop their proficiency in English.

Reflections is designed to support students' efforts to develop their skills under the guidance of instructors who:

— Know how important it is to start where students are in their use of language.
— Understand the importance of drawing on the varied backgrounds, interests and experiences the students bring with them to the class.
— Recognize that students come to class with widely varying goals and are ready to adapt the program to help them achieve these goals.
— Believe that students learn English best by communicating with others in a real-world context.
— Encourage discussion and debate, knowing that this helps create the kind of interactive learning environment that fosters language growth.
— Are eager to introduce students to a variety of excellent literature, designed to stimulate a wide range of interests.
— Understand that students need practical tools and terminology to help them refine the English-language skills they already possess.
— Support students' efforts to take responsibility for their own learning by establishing a classroom atmosphere that encourages this.

As a result, this guide is exactly that—a guide to, not a step-by-step blueprint for, using *Reflections*. It assumes that instructors will be selective, picking and choosing, and adapting and refining the ideas, activity suggestions and exercises to match the varied backgrounds, learning styles, goals, needs, interests and abilities of the students. It is not necessary to "do" every activity in every unit, nor are the units designed to be taught in lock-step fashion, with students laboriously working their way through the exercises one by one; rather, it's expected that you will use *Reflections*—and this guide—as a springboard to developing your own creative approaches to the curriculum.

To help with this process, a variety of strategies for approaching specific elements of the units are included in this guide. These suggestions are here, not to prescribe how the units *must* be taught, but rather as a source of ideas for priming your own idea pump.

HOW *REFLECTIONS* IS ORGANIZED

Reflections is presented in two parts. The first 13 units contain readings from selected literature accompanied by suggestions for related oral and written activities; the remaining 12 units are devoted to oral activities, though most also include suggestions for written follow-up. For quick reference, charts outlining the themes, issues and activities covered in the units begin each section. There is also an index setting out the grammar and vocabulary topics covered.

Part 1: Readings and Reading Activities

The Reading Passages

The readings in this section of *Reflections* are designed to introduce students to a variety of authors and genres—fiction, non-fiction, drama, poetry, journalism and essays. After each selection, there is a note about the author that includes, when appropriate, the historical, cultural or political context of the reading. When approaching some readings, it may be useful to draw students' attention to the biographical note *before* beginning to read the passage. Unit 13, a scene from Rod Langley's play, *Bethune*, is an example: it's essential for students to understand the context before they read the scene.

The readings can be approached in a variety of ways, depending on the students' needs, interests, abilities and learning styles. In many cases, for example, they are short enough to be read aloud in class by the instructor or by the students taking turns, or both. To ensure that students have an opportunity to appreciate the work as a creative whole, it's sometimes a good idea to read the entire passage before any discussion takes place. In some instances, you may wish to guide the students' reading by suggesting that they read either the entire selection or predefined passages "to find out…," a technique that helps focus and give purpose to their reading. In other instances, introducing a passage using a directed reading-thinking activity (see p. 9) can help students draw on their previous knowledge to stimulate understanding and discussion.

Activities

In most cases, the activities that follow each reading are organized under five headings: comprehension, discussion, vocabulary building, writing and grammar. In addition, many of the units include follow-up suggestions that can be used to extend the students' experiences with the theme of the passage.

COMPREHENSION

These questions are intended to help guide the students' reading of the passage, check their understanding, draw their attention to unusual or difficult words, expressions and concepts, and stimulate discussion in conjunction with a close reading of the text.

Rather than working your way through the questions one by one, it's a good idea to review them beforehand and, based on your knowledge of the students, select those that are appropriate.

For example, you might read the first paragraph, then ask a question about what has been read. In this way, the questions become a natural and integral part of the class, one that arises spontaneously from the students' encounter with the text. If you weave the questions into a general discussion of the passage, you will probably find that you have covered the whole exercise quite painlessly.

DISCUSSION

These questions are designed to stimulate discussion of the passage. Again, you know the students best and are in the best position to decide which to emphasize—and when.

In many cases, it works well to divide the class into groups of two or three, assigning a different topic to each group. When the discussion ends, a spokesperson for each group can summarize its findings for the class, a strategy that may extend the discussions considerably.

VOCABULARY BUILDING

Depending on the needs of the students, these activities may be covered orally or in writing. In some cases, the exercises may be assigned as homework or for study by the students on their own. This works particularly well with exercises that ask students to match highlighted words in sentences with a list of synonyms. Just photocopy the answers from this guide and encourage the students to check their own work.

WRITING

The writing assignments vary in purpose and difficulty. The way you choose to use them will depend very much on the expectations you and the students have for written English. For example, if your goal is simply to provide students with opportunities to practise their written English and gain confidence in their ability to express their ideas, you may not wish to go beyond the specific assignment. If, however, the students are preparing for a program in which formal writing is required, you may wish to stress the mechanics of essay-writing and assess students' efforts accordingly. In most cases, the writing assignments can be adapted to both purposes.

No matter what goals you and the students set for their writing, using portfolios (see p. 11) is an excellent strategy for developing their awareness of writing as a process and encouraging them to become actively involved in assessing their own progress.

GRAMMAR

The grammar exercises accompanying each unit are designed for students who are ready to go beyond the basics. Depending on the students' needs, they may be completed in class—orally or in writing—or assigned as homework. Because many of the concepts covered are fairly sophisticated, however, it's a good idea to review them before handing out the assignment, whether it's to be completed in or out of class. By the same token, be prepared to discuss students' answers in class, helping them through any difficulties they may encounter.

Part 2: Oral Activities

The 12 units in this section are designed to offer students opportunities to put their growing proficiency in spoken English to work in real-world contexts. Each unit presents a situation, which is often very complex precisely so that it will spark lively discussion and debate, then suggests oral activities that provide an authentic framework for this discussion. In many cases, writing and follow-up activities that extend the theme are also suggested.

While all the oral units can certainly stand alone, some relate very well to specific themes introduced in the reading passages. When this is the case, the relationship is noted in this guide.

Even when your emphasis is on written English, the oral units are useful. The scenarios provide reading practice, while the activities can help introduce writing tasks that reinforce those found in Part 1.

To provide a model for organizing and working with the oral units, Unit 15—Short-Term Gain, Long-Term Pain? (p. 85)—is presented in more detail than the other selections in this section of the guide. Again, this model is provided as a source of ideas and inspiration, and is not intended to limit the creative techniques and strategies you use. Feel free to adapt the ideas to fit the needs of the students in your class and your own teaching style.

TEACHING STRATEGIES

Directed Reading-Thinking Activity

Drawing on students' previous knowledge and experience helps them understand a passage by relating what they already know to what they are reading. It's often difficult, however, for students whose first language is not English to do this. While they may be able to talk about an experience in their home language, they are sometimes at loss to do the same in English. In addition, they may be accustomed to relying on the instructor for direction, without realizing that they can make their own predictions about and monitor their own understanding of unknown material.

The directed reading-thinking activity encourages students to make predictions about unfamiliar reading material, then confirm or reject these predictions. Doing so reduces their dependence on the instructor, builds their confidence in themselves as readers and speakers of English and encourages them to make their own meaning out of text.

Because it's relatively short, accompanied by a photograph, and contains a wonderful element of surprise, "A Traveller's Tale" is an excellent vehicle for introducing DRTAs.

Beforehand, read the story yourself and decide on several logical stopping points. In the case of "A Traveller's Tale," these stopping points might occur after the first paragraph, the second paragraph, the third, the sixth, and at the end of the story.

In class, invite students to turn to the story, look at the photograph and read the title. Remind them not to read ahead. To prevent this, suggest that they use blank sheets of paper to cover the text.

Ask the following questions:

— What do you think this story is about?
— What makes you think so?

Record students' predictions in point form on the chalkboard. As with any brainstorming activity, it's important to accept all responses. Everyone is experimenting and there are no "right" answers.

Next, invite students to uncover the author's name. Then, ask the same two questions. In this case, it's unlikely that knowing John Fraser's name will affect their predictions; however, think about how your own predictions might change if you discovered the author was Jules Verne.

Now, invite the students to uncover and silently read the first paragraph. At this point, your questions change slightly. Ask:

— What do you think will happen next?
— Why do you think so?

Continue this way, stopping at the predetermined points and asking only these questions, until you reach the end of the story. Avoid the temptation to throw in comprehension questions to check students' understanding. Save these for later.

Once the DRTA is finished, interweave a discussion of the students' predictions with some of the questions outlined in the Comprehension section of *Reflections*.

DRTAs can be used effectively with short stories and to introduce some longer reading passages. Like any other technique, however, they can be overused so that their appeal quickly palls. When a selection in *Reflections* is particularly well-suited to using a DRTA, this is noted in the pre-reading suggestions.

Writing Portfolios

By acknowledging that writing is a process, this strategy, too, reduces students' dependence on the instructor and encourages them to become actively involved in and share responsibility for their own progress.

The portfolio itself is just that—a portfolio, often a file folder, in which students store their writing. In many cases, the folder is divided into three sections—one for ideas, a second for work in progress, and a third for finished pieces.

At the beginning of each course, prepare a file folder for each student. On the inside front cover, attach a course schedule with the date of every class. This enables you to check off assignments as they're collected. In addition, provide space for recording progress on and due dates for other writing activities—outline, first draft, revisions, rewriting and so on. This serves as a gentle reminder to tardy students that work is due.

There is debate over who—the instructor or the students—should keep track of the portfolios. On the one hand, an instructor who keeps all the portfolios and collects and files daily writing and assignments may seem overly controlling. On the other, when the instructor keeps the portfolios, it minimizes the risk that they will be lost and enables you to review students' work at your own pace.

No matter what tracking process you decide to use, however, the portfolio is more than simply a system for storing writing samples. The key to using it effectively is to transfer control of the process to the students. Often, in consultation with the instructor and their peers, students decide which ideas they wish to pursue, which work in progress they want to polish, and which of the finished pieces are their "best." In many cases, it is these that are submitted for formal evaluation, a process that often involves students' own assessment, as well as that of their peers and the instructor.

An important element of the portfolio approach is the conference, which is an opportunity for the instructor to get together with individual students to review their goals and discuss their progress. For this reason, it's a good idea to encourage students not to throw away any work. Every piece of writing is valuable, as it enables students to see their writing as a continuing process. Nothing is wasted; halting first attempts can, if the student wishes and time permits, evolve into more polished writing.

When students confer with you about their progress, the portfolio enables them to ask for your advice in the context of their whole body of work. Too often, students focus on how their grades on isolated assignments compare with those of their peers. The portfolio helps shift the emphasis toward a student's personal development. Together, you and the student can set realistic, individual goals for improving writing.

The portfolio approach can be adapted to a variety of purposes in a variety of programs. Some suggestions follow.

Free-Writing

You might find it interesting to give students an opportunity to do some free-writing during the first 10 to 20 minutes of each class. At this point, stress that quantity—rather than quality—is the objective. The only "rule" is that students must write, even if it is to say that they don't know what to write about.

Free-writing enables students to explore ideas that pop into their heads without fear of being "corrected." Some instructors collect this writing every day, and place it in the students' portfolios. Though you can check that the writing has been done, it's a good idea not to read their entries—at this point.

At first, some students may prefer to be assigned a writing topic. This may be a prelude to a reading, or something suggested by a reading done in class or the daily news, or even something totally whimsical. However, if you decide to assign topics, invite students to suggest their own every so often—and write along with them!

Two or three times during the course, invite students to review their free-writing entries and select three to hand in for marking. If they wish, they may polish their entries at this point.

During individual conferences, skim all the free-writing entries, and ask students what makes the three they have chosen their "best." This open-ended discussion is often very revealing.

Formal Writing Tasks

In addition to free-writing, the class will be working on more formal writing tasks, such as those included in each unit of *Reflections*. Students' portfolios might contain outlines and rough drafts of this work in progress, as well as finished pieces and previously graded work.

Supplementary Reading

Instructors often encourage students to read English-language books and other materials outside of class. The portfolio can include a worksheet of activities on this segment of the course, to be completed by a certain deadline. This enables students to work at their own pace, consulting you if difficulties arise.

Mix and Match

Feel free to choose whatever aspect of the portfolio approach suits your own teaching style. You don't have to embrace it as *the* way to manage the course. If this is your first venture in using portfolios, you might consider trying them for one component of the course only—free-writing, for example. If they work well, you'll find other applications appropriate to the students' needs.

Brainstorming

Brainstorming sessions are most effective when it's acknowledged that *everyone* is experimenting and, therefore, feels free to express themselves. This is particularly important when working with ESL students whose previous experience may be in classrooms where only "correct" answers were acceptable, or who may be reluctant to speak up because they believe their English skills are inadequate or their contributions will be ridiculed. Don't be discouraged if some of your early sessions are less than successful. It takes time for some students to get used to the idea that *all* contributions are welcomed.

    The instructor plays a very important role in fostering an environment that encourages free expression and ensures that everyone has an opportunity to contribute. One of the best ways of doing this is to model supportive behavior by accepting and recording all ideas in a non-judgmental fashion. When it's necessary to edit a statement, check with the speaker before changing his or her words. This helps students internalize the message that their ideas are respected.

    You'll know you've been successful when students begin using the techniques you've modelled as they're working on their own in groups. Occasionally, however, it may be necessary to provide direct instruction in the techniques of brainstorming, making explicit what's involved and why.

Groupwork

Many of the activities suggested in *Reflections* involve students in groupwork, another strategy that reduces their reliance on the instructor. In ESL classrooms, it's often a good idea to limit groups to three members to ensure that everyone has an opportunity to discover that they have a contribution to make. Forming larger groups increases the likelihood that one or two personalities will dominate, overwhelming the efforts of those who may express themselves less confidently.

To keep students focused on the group assignment, it helps to explain that each group is expected to appoint a spokesperson to report its findings to the class. As the spokespersons report, provide students from other groups with an opportunity to add their own observations, a technique that often sparks lively whole-class discussions.

When students are engaged in groupwork, instructors play a variety of important roles. If one group is bogged down, for example, the instructor can sit in for a few minutes and model techniques for getting over the obstacle. In some cases, this may involve providing the vocabulary students need to interpret ideas effectively or even suggesting ideas to revive a flagging discussion. On the other hand, if many of the groups are having similar problems, it may signal the need for a whole-class mini-lesson on a particular aspect of group dynamics.

Groupwork gives instructors an opportunity to observe the language growth of individual students in a more relaxed setting. How well is an individual participating? Is a student applying skills or principles that have been learned formally to her work in a group? Often, it helps to keep anecdotal records of these observations, which can be discussed with students during individual conferences. At the same time, they can also reveal a need to introduce or review specific language concepts with the entire class.

Part 1
Readings and Reading Activities

VERB TENSES AT A GLANCE

TENSE	FORMATION	SOME TIME SIGNALS	USE	EXAMPLES
Simple Present	Root form (3rd person adds S) Auxiliary: do, does	Every day (week, etc.), on Mondays, etc.	Expresses habitual action… or timeless condition.	I usually **drink** tea. I **don't like** spiders.
Present Continuous	BE (conjugated) + root form + ING	Now, at this moment, etc.	Describes action that is occurring at the same time as the words are spoken.	I **am working** at Eaton's these days. **Is** Rashid **eating** dinner at the moment?
Simple Past	Regular: root form + ED Irregular: past form must be memorized (e.g., go/went/gone) Auxiliary: did	Last week, a week ago, etc.	Expresses completed action that occurred at a definite time. Tells when.	I **visited** Russia last year. **Did** you **have** a good time last night?
Present Perfect	HAS or HAVE + past participle	Since, for Adverbs of frequency: often, never, etc.	Expresses action begun in the past and continuing in the present… or indefinite time: tells how many times, how often.	I **have lived** in Toronto for six years (since 1988). Marco **has seen** *Wolf* twice. **Have** you **eaten** yet?
Present Perfect Continuous	HAS BEEN or HAVE BEEN + present participle	Since, for, until now, etc.	Emphasizes the duration of the action or state. Does *not* express indefinite time.	I **have been studying** since four o'clock. It **has been raining** all day.
Past Continuous	WAS or WERE + present participle	While (during the same time that), as (at the same time as)	Expresses action that interrupts another action… or occurs at the same time as another action.	George fell as he **was crossing** the street. You phoned while I **was having** a bath.

VERB TENSES AT A GLANCE

TENSE	FORMATION	SOME TIME SIGNALS	USE	EXAMPLES
Past Perfect	HAD + past participle	Before, after, by the time, until (specific time)	Expresses a completed action that occurred *before* another completed action in the past. Often used to express tense in indirect speech: tells how long. Used in past unreal conditions.	By the time Roland arrived, we **had finished** dinner. Until last Christmas, Lan **had never seen** snow. If you **had studied**, you would have passed.
Past Perfect Continuous	HAD BEEN + present participle	Before, when, not…until	Emphasizes the duration of an action or state that continues up to a *definite* time in the past.	John **had been trying** to call the the hospital for some time before the ambulance arrived.
Simple Future	SHALL or WILL + root form IS, AM, ARE GOING TO + root form	Tomorrow, next week (month), etc.	Expresses future action—prediction: use **will** or **be going to**. prior plan: use **be going to** only. willingness: use **will** only	You **will be** sick is you don't rest. You're **going to be** sick if… I'm **going to phone** Li on Sunday. It's cold. I'll **close** the window.
Continuous Future	SHALL BE or WILL BE + present participle	*At* a specified time in the future.	Expresses continuous action that will take place *at* or *up to* a specific time in the future.	John **will be working** until six o'clock. I **shall be taking** a nap when you arrive.
Future Perfect	SHALL HAVE or WILL HAVE + past participle	*By* a specified time in the future.	Expresses action that will occur or be completed before another future event.	By next summer, George **will have completed** his degree.
Future Perfect Continuous	SHALL HAVE BEEN or WILL HAVE BEEN + present participle	*By* a specified time in the future	Expresses a continuous action that will take place until the time of another future event.	By the time you cross the finish line, you **will have been running** for four hours.

UNIT 1
A Traveller's Tale

PRE-READING

Invite students to imagine that they are planning a holiday in a foreign country. How would they prepare for the trip? What meaning does the word "foreign" convey?

These questions are designed to lead to a discussion of a foreign country as one that is far-off in distance, language and, in all likelihood, culture. Guide the discussion toward considering how we might prepare to encounter a different culture and whether it is the traveller's—or the host country's—responsibility to ensure that everything goes smoothly.

An alternative is to use a DRTA (see p. 9) to introduce this story.

COMPREHENSION

1. By and large, these details provide emphasis and color, and help set the stage for what is to come.

    When discussing *c*, draw students' attention to the inverted word order "had she" after the negative expression at the beginning of the sentence. Show them other examples, such as:

    Never (seldom, not often) have I been so insulted.
    Not only were they late, but they were also tiresome.

    In *i*, the word "Western" provides an important clue for readers, suggesting that ours is not the only way of thinking about privacy.
2. A Western reader probably identifies with the French woman. We assume that her actions are perfectly natural, and empathize with her embarrassment at the floor boy's unexpected entry.
3. We expect the manager to apologize for the boy's behavior.
4. The impersonal construction maintains the element of surprise by drawing readers more deeply into the cultural misunderstanding.

5. These words can be interpreted two ways. Do they signal that something is about to cause the woman's enthusiasm for China to change? Or, do they simply emphasize what's about to happen next?
6. The absence of a verb in this "sentence" indicates that there is no action. The state of things is being described. That this is a separate paragraph emphasizes the silence—and gives readers the first strong hint that all may not be as we thought.
7. Because we identify with the young French woman, we overlook the clues John Fraser presents as the story unfolds. We are lulled into making the same cultural mistake as the woman, and are completely surprised by the manager's criticism. At the end, we laugh somewhat ruefully because the joke is on us.

DISCUSSION

Privacy

These questions are open-ended, designed to guide students toward an awareness of cultural assumptions about privacy.

Home

These sayings about home are designed to introduce students to familiar English quotations. Encourage students to come up with other sayings about home, drawn perhaps from their own cultures.

The final quotation, number 5, deals with a family's duties toward its members. In this case, home is described as a place we can return to if circumstances force us to. Our family has a duty to take us in.

Encourage a debate on this view of home.

In Robert Frost's poem, "The Death of the Hired Man," from which this quote is taken, Silas, an old man who is sick and unable to work, arrives at the farm of a young couple for whom he has worked somewhat unreliably in the past. Mary wants to let Silas stay with them till he dies. Warren insists that Silas seek refuge with his own family, whose duty it is to take him in. The quoted words, spoken by Warren, deal with this obligation.

Mary disagrees and, in the next lines, argues, "I should have called it (home)/Something you somehow haven't to deserve." She believes that home is the place where we are accepted unconditionally, out of love and compassion.

VOCABULARY BUILDING

1. weary
2. emerged
3. warning
4. procedure
5. conception
6. permitted
7. outweigh
8. startled
9. abashed
10. extricating

WRITING

1. The point here is to separate what actually happened from an interpretation of the events, then to color the story with the emotions experienced by the various participants.
   a. The French woman may be embarrassed by the incident, and think badly of China as a result. She may realize that she should have been more sensitive to cultural differences, and chalk it up to experience. Or, she may be angry and unwilling to accept any responsibility for the misunderstanding.
   b. The floor boy may simply be upset by his bizarre encounter. Or, he may realize that people from other countries have different customs, and resolve to be more cautious in future.
   c. The manager's version will probably include some frustration at having to deal with such an odd occurrence. While he wants to accommodate the hotel's foreign guests and provide excellent service, he must also uphold standards of decency and ensure that employees are not subjected to such shocking behavior. On the other hand, he may show a lack of understanding of Western culture, and an unwillingness to make allowances for the French woman's ignorance of Chinese ways.
2. This assignment enables students to be personal and creative.

GRAMMAR

It might be useful to photocopy "Verb Tenses at a Glance" on pages 16-17 of this guide and distribute these pages to students.

Verb Tenses

1. seems
2. is
3. had begun (was beginning)
4. had developed

5. (had) continued
6. ended
7. came
8. adopted
9. included
10. accepted
11. to teach
12. lived (were living)
13. encountered
14. were (had been)
15. went
16. attracted
17. wanted
18. were buying (had bought)
19. had (never) seen
20. touched
21. were
22. have (you) eaten
23. are
24. had had (has had)
25. made (makes)
26. was balanced
27. lived
28. worked
29. were
30. would (not) change

It may be necessary to help students understand that the tense used for the first verb in a complex sentence dictates the tense that *must* be used for the second. In addition, many students may use the simple past instead of the past perfect, especially in numbers 3, 4, 5, 14, 18 and 24. If so, point out that they may indeed hear the simple past more often than the past perfect, and offer them a reason.

Here's an example:
He said he had finished his homework.

We often abbreviate this to:
He said he'd finished his homework.

Because it is very difficult to hear this abbreviation, it is a short step to omitting it altogether, so we often hear:
He said he finished his homework.

For the purposes of this book, the past perfect is included when a strict application of the rules demands it.

Prepositions

1. after (upon, on)
2. to
3. at
4. in
5. in
6. for
7. on (to)
8. of (to)
9. in
10. at
11. into
12. without
13. in
14. to

15. into
16. in
17. of
18. by
19. to
20. by
21. for
22. with
23. of
24. on, upon

SENTENCE COMBINING

1. While the young woman was having a bath, the floor boy entered the room.
   The floor boy entered the room while the young woman was having a bath.
2. The young French woman did not blame the floor boy although he entered her room without knocking.
   Although the floor boy entered her room without knocking, the young French woman did not blame him.
3. The manager said that the floor boy would have to go home to recover. (You can point out that we often omit the subordinate conjunction "that" and say, "The manager said the floor boy....")
4. There has been an incident because you did not observe the rules of decency.
5. The young woman was full of enthusiasm for China before she was criticized by the hotel manager. (We could also say, "The young woman was full of enthusiasm for China before being criticized by the hotel manager." Here, however, "before" is a preposition rather than a subordinate conjunction.)

FOLLOW-UP

The activities in Unit 24—Who's at Fault?—provide an excellent opportunity to extend some of the concepts and themes introduced in this unit.

UNIT 2

A Visitor

PRE-READING

A DRTA (see p. 9) may be used to introduce this sketch.

Invite students to compare the following synonyms and near-synonyms: guest, visitor, tourist, caller, company. What connotations are suggested by the word "visitor"?

Or, suggest that students look at the photograph on page 24 of *Reflections*, then free-write about what it evokes.

COMPREHENSION

1. The visitor is Death.
2. We can infer that the woman is in a coma.
3. Winter is traditionally associated with dying. Carr sets the story in spring, the season often associated with rebirth and new life. Carr's choice of this season suggests that this death is not fearful, but beautiful, in keeping with the gentleness of nature at this time of year.
4. The woman accepts her death; she does not fight against it. Perhaps she is old, and has enjoyed a long and fulfilling life. Perhaps she has been ill and sees her death as a release from pain, suffering and the guilt she feels at burdening others.
5. Out of respect for the woman's approaching death, human noise has been reduced to a minimum; in the silence, we suddenly notice background noises that we don't normally hear. The ticking clock emphasizes the passing of time as a life runs out.
6. At the moment of death, the woman's face still bears the imprint of her personality and registers her gladness to be gone. Then, all traces of her spirit leave her body, which becomes simply an empty shell that needs to be buried.
7. At the funeral, they are sad for themselves because the woman has left them.

8. To the undertakers, handling the coffin is simply a job. Their only interest is in how difficult it is to get it down the stairs.
9. After the woman's death, the house is a place in which every stage of life has been celebrated: birth, marriage and death. The house experiences these stages of a human lifetime in a very short period—a single year.
10. Perhaps Carr wishes to underscore our link with the natural world. The boundary between life and death, animate and inanimate, is sometimes not clearly perceived and may not be as absolute as we usually believe.

DISCUSSION

These questions are open-ended, designed to guide students toward an awareness of different cultural attitudes toward death; for example, reincarnation, ancestor worship, belief in an after-life, and so on. You may wish to guide students toward a discussion of the fact that many Western cultures tend to sanitize death, by moving it to another location—the hospital—and hiring undertakers to handle the body and funeral arrangements. This may lead to a comparison of funeral rituals in various cultures.

Before discussing the alternative expressions for death and dying, it might be useful to consider euphemisms. Why do we feel the need to soften the language we use to talk about death? What other topics call for euphemisms?

You might invite students to come up with a list of less reverent or tasteful expressions describing death, such as:

Emily has kicked the bucket.
She is pushing up the daisies.

Encourage a discussion of why we sometimes use these expressions.

VOCABULARY BUILDING

Two-Word Adjectives
1. user-friendly computer products
2. feather-light pastry
3. waist-high water

4. knee-high socks (knee socks or knee-highs)
5. a razor-sharp knife
6. steel-grey eyes
7. a microwave-safe plate
8. ice-cold beer
9. static-free clothes
10. sugar-free cola

WRITING

Students may need guidance in writing an essay that involves comparing and contrasting. A suggestion is included for each topic.

1. Begin by inviting students to free-write about society's view of death. Then, encourage them to suggest points from their writing as you record them on the chalkboard. Work on the list until the class is satisfied that it is complete. Ask students to formulate a statement summarizing the way our society views death.

   Then, go through the list, asking whether Carr's portrayal of death conforms to or departs from each point. Encourage students to back up their responses by referring to specific details in the story. Conclude by suggesting that the class formulate a statement describing Carr's view of death. The two statements can then be combined into an opening paragraph for the essay. Assign the first draft for homework.

2. Invite the class to work in pairs. One person lists the benefits of dying at home; the other, the benefits of dying in a hospital. Students compare their lists and discuss the benefits and drawbacks of each setting. Each student can decide whether one choice significantly outweighs the other, or whether it is a matter to be decided by the individual. If necessary, you might help students construct effective opening statements.

GRAMMAR

The Conditional

Note that the students' answers may not precisely match the wording given here. The importance of this exercise lies in using the conditional correctly.

1. ...she had been afraid.
2. ...the parson had not spoken in such a sad voice.
3. ...she would not have had a smile on her face.
4. ...someone dies there.
5. ...will be able to smell the spring flowers.
6. ...we had been so quiet around her.
7. ...she had not asked to be taken away.
8. ...would not have cried.
9. ...the stairs had been really difficult to negotiate.
10. ...were sure that is what he wants.

Sentence Structure

There may be more than one way of combining these sentences.

1. Many people avoid going to the doctor although they are often very ill.
2. My aunt refuses to go to the hospital because she thinks she will die there.
3. Nurses who care for the terminally ill are very dedicated.
4. When my son played basketball last summer, he broke two fingers.
5. Although his hand was in a cast, he continued to play basketball.
6. Death was waiting for the person who lay in my spare room.
7. One end of the coffin rested on the big table on which people had heaped flowers.
8. We cried while the parson was talking in a low, sad voice.
9. When it became time for her to leave our house, the undertaker took her away in a hearse.
10. We could not be sad for her because she had welcomed Death.

FOLLOW-UP

If they're available, show prints of some of Emily Carr's paintings. It may be interesting to ask whether students see a connection between Carr's artistic vision of nature and her acceptance of death in "A Visitor." Invite the class to bring in pictures representing death.

If time and interest permit, you might introduce John Donne's poem, "Death Be Not Proud," Dylan Thomas's "Do Not Go Gentle into That Good Night," or William Wordsworth's "We Are Seven." You might also invite the class to bring in music that depicts death.

UNIT 3

Going for the Gold

PRE-READING

Draw students' attention to the picture on page 32 and ask questions such as:

— What does the woman's body language communicate? What kind of person does she seem to be?
— What kind of job might she do, and how do we know?

This can be a group discussion activity or a free-writing exercise.
Alternatively, invite students to free-write about one of the following topics:

— How do you handle stress in your life.
— Is it society's responsibility to guarantee everyone a job?

COMPREHENSION

1. This article was written in 1993 when the economy was in a recession and the unemployment rate was high.
2. Many tasks that used to be performed manually are now automated: sorting mail, operating a telephone switchboard, low-skilled assembly-line jobs, billing, payroll and so on. With reduced numbers of employees, there is also a reduction in the number of middle managers needed.
3. "People skills" refers to our ability to deal harmoniously with the people we encounter. For example, Oriana may use humor to put her boss in a good mood.
4. Ruth's clothes, hair and makeup need to be tailored, professional, well-cut and elegant—probably classic chic rather than high-fashion—to enhance her image as a businessperson.

5. When you are the boss, there are probably fewer co-workers with whom you can be friends; employees who report to you must be kept at a certain professional distance. As a result, you may be lonely. However, because your salary is higher, you "eat better."
6. The term "glass ceiling" refers to the invisible barriers that prevent advancement. A person who believes that she won't be promoted no matter how well she performs may not work as enthusiastically; if this happens, the glass ceiling may become a reality, even if it didn't exist in the first place.
7. An entrepreneurial approach involves welcoming new ideas and taking risks while a bureaucratic approach involves a hierarchical structure that discourages these qualities.
8. A go-getter is an aggressively enterprising person; "smarts" is mental alertness, the ability to respond intelligently; "put your money where your mouth is" means that you're prepared to back your judgment by risking your personal assets.
9. We need to find exactly the right amount of challenge in our job. We can cope with work-related stress by identifying the stressor. If we can fix it, wonderful; if not, we can practise stress-management techniques.
10. With its "snapshots" and sidebars, this article can be read in bits and pieces, in no particular order, a format that suits the busy person. Newspapers use a similar format. On the other hand, a magazine such as *Reader's Digest* tends to be more linear as the articles present information or tell a story. Books, too, are usually linear to prevent readers from getting lost.

DISCUSSION

1. It is interesting to hear students' perceptions of high-stress jobs. They may conclude that stress is caused equally by jobs that are varied, challenging and carry a high degree of responsibility, and jobs that are routine, boring and without responsibility for or opportunities to influence decision-making.
2. Many people don't perceive that blue-collar jobs carry the same status as white-collar jobs. Because we tend to equate status with money, we may be surprised by the discrepancy.
3. Opinions will vary.

4. This question may spark an interesting discussion of feminism and employment equity.
5. If job specifications continue to change at the current rate, much of what students learn in school may be obsolete by the time they graduate. The current shift in education, then, is away from content-based education to skills-based, or competency-based, learning. According to current research, the ability to think clearly and critically, solve problems and work co-operatively across linguistic and cultural boundaries is a prized skill in the job market. Discuss this idea with the class, then ask what skills they think they will need to prepare for the future.

VOCABULARY BUILDING

Encountering New Words, A Personal Word List

Talk about the information in this section, then suggest that students start personal word lists. Regularly set aside a few minutes to ask students to share words or expressions they have encountered.

Vocabulary Alternatives

1. ...refrain from raising an issue that does not absolutely require me to act.
2. ...a benefit that is available right now is worth more than a larger benefit that may—or may not—be received in the future.
3. ...the only available or qualified person.
4. ...terrific.
5. ...achieving two objectives at once.
6. ...a very small portion of a much larger but less obvious whole.
7. ...not to count on something before it actually comes to pass.

Just for Fun

"Snail-mail" is regular surface mail. A "mouse potato" is someone who spends too much time with computers—with a mouse.

WRITING

1. This is a straightforward piece of imaginative writing.
2. The suggestions in Unit 2 (see p. 25) apply equally well to this assignment.

3. This creative piece requires students to follow a logical path.
4. Because this topic is somewhat abstract, students may need guidance. Introduce the assignment by discussing the limitations of training for specific jobs in a world where traditional jobs are disappearing. Encourage students to talk about the skills they think are necessary for life-long learning.

GRAMMAR

Modals

Answers will vary.

Relative Pronouns and Relative Adverbs

1. Lynn earns a good hourly wage, which her membership in a union helps to ensure.
2. Cultivate mentors in your field from whom you can ask advice.
3. I have decided to take a word processing course that includes desktop publishing.
4. Oriana has a 45-minute commute on the Skytrain to downtown Vancouver where she works.
5. Many of Lise's clients who are being investigated for child abuse and neglect are unco-operative.
6. My daughter is looking forward to the future when jobs such as underwater archeologist will be common.
7. Micheline works for a Montreal computer consulting company where she is vice-president of marketing.
8. Oriana feels that her "people skills," which she has developed over the years, will give her an edge.
9. I asked Oriana why landing a teaching job might be difficult for her.
10. Anyone who possesses the self-discipline and emotional fortitude to work alone at home might be an excellent candidate for the so-called "open collar" sector.

FOLLOW-UP

Unit 23—The Best Candidate—makes an excellent follow-up to the theme of this article.

UNIT 4

The Day It Rained Forever

PRE-READING

Suggest that students free-write on one of the following topics:

— Rain
— To what extent does weather affect your mood?
— What feelings are evoked by the photo on page 48 of *Reflections*?

COMPREHENSION

1. The writer liked the sound of the rain falling on the roof, the sweet smell in the air and the playful swaying of the coconut trees in the breeze on rainy days in Bangladesh.
2. In this case, a synonym for "would" is "used to."
3. There are numerous possibilities: sizzle, crash, thump, whisper and words representing animal noises—meow, moo etc.
4. The rain was so heavy and uncomfortable that the writer could not imagine that a human being would be out in it.
5. The enormity of the little boy's plight made anything she might have said seem inadequate. His situation was so far removed from her own and contrasted so sharply with her previous thoughts about the beauty of rain that she felt foolish. She may even have felt a little guilty for being so unaware of the day-to-day concerns of someone who had recently been a neighbor.
6. The little boy's words about his hopes and dreams fell from his heart in a steady stream like raindrops from the sky.
7. His dream is just like that of any other little boy anywhere in the world. It transcends economic and cultural barriers.
8. A stone's throw away is a very short distance away.
9. Now, she realizes that rain can be destructive as well as life-giving and that many people's lives are totally dependent on the whims of nature. In the opening sentence, she uses the past

31

perfect tense, "I had always loved rainy days," to suggest that her feelings changed after the incident described in the story.
10. This is an open-ended question that should spark lively debate. Some students may see the story simply as a "slice of life." Others may see it as a significant social awakening for the author. Still others may attach a moral to it.

DISCUSSION

1. Encourage students to discuss how wealth and extreme poverty are handled in a developing country such as Bangladesh. Another privileged young person might have sent the child away, or given him a small sum of money—*baksheesh*—so that he would leave. We see that Hamidullah is compassionate and sensitive, willing to learn more about the world around her, even if this makes her uncomfortable.
2. This dialogue requires students to step briefly into the characters' shoes and see the privileged from the point of view of the impoverished. Abdul may be pleased that the writer has listened to his story, surprised that she understands so little, or scornful that she is so naive; his sister may be resigned to, cynical or even bitter about the inequity in their social stations, and so on.
3. In the writer's imagination, the rain seemed to be the giver of beauty, "mysterious and romantic." The child introduced her to another dimension of the rain: the nourisher—and destroyer—of the crops that provide the peasants' livelihood. Yet the rain also serves as "matchmaker," bringing Hamidullah and the child together in a conversation that leads to understanding—at least for the author.
4. Encourage students to discuss the meaning of these proverbs and quotations, and add some of their own.

VOCABULARY BUILDING

Synonyms
1. grumble
2. quenched
3. assuming
4. scrutinizing
5. anxiety
6. deserted

7. pebbles
8. salvage
9. soothing
10. countless

Figurative Language
Answers will vary.

WRITING

1. This assignment can be handled in much the same way as the writing assignments in Unit 2 (see p. 25 of this guide).
2. This assignment requires the writer to be aware of her audience. Begin by inviting students to list arguments for and against taking a year off school in order to travel. Then help them turn their attention to the potential reader. What is the purpose of the letter? To offer support and encouragement? To dissuade? What is the reader like—shy, outgoing, stubborn, etc.? What arguments are most likely to be effective with this person?

    Discuss how a writer's awareness of her audience and a clear idea of her purpose help determine the content of her arguments and suggest the most effective style or tone to adopt.

    It might be useful to have students compare their letters.
3. This topic is more difficult, as it is abstract and somewhat academic. Begin by defining irony. In terms of Hamidullah's story, the most useful definition might be incongruity between what might be expected to happen and what actually does happen.

GRAMMAR

Verbs: Modals

In many cases, there is more than one appropriate answer. However, it is useful to talk about the shade of meaning each possibility conveys. This helps students become aware of the need to vary their word choice to avoid repetition.

1. can
2. should, would
3. must, should
4. might, may
5. must, should, ought to
6. can
7. must, have to
8. may, might
9. may
10. should, ought to

11. can, may, might
12. may, might, could
13. can, will be able to
14. must, have to
15. should, ought to, might
16. should, ought to
17. might, could
18. should, ought to, must
19. must, have to, should
20. should, ought to

Sentence Combining

Again, in many cases, there is more than one correct answer.

1. While other children grumbled about staying home, I found the rain mysterious and romantic.
2. Although the rain fell continuously for three months, I never became tired of it.
3. As I was standing on the balcony, the falling rain felt like stinging nettles on my skin.
4. The boy's shirt was so old that one could barely make out the number 10 on it.
5. I ran back from school in the afternoon to watch cartoons on TV.
6. He patiently explained to me that the farmers had a love-hate relationship with the rain.
7. The same rain that caused the floods nourished the rice fields.
8. This boy knew many things about life, although he had received no formal education.
9. A thousand thoughts rushed through my head as I drifted off to sleep.
10. I thought of the countless others who sang and cried in the rain.

FOLLOW-UP

Invite students to bring in references to rain in songs, poems, paintings, photographs and so on. Use their material for a free-flowing discussion of the cultural and symbolic attributes of rain, and the extent to which weather plays a part in our lives.

UNIT 5

Human Rights and Human Responsibilities

PRE-READING

Suggest that students free-write on one of the following topics:

— What is the difference between rights and responsibilities?
— Should we give money to beggars? Why or why not?

COMPREHENSION

The first nine questions will encourage students to revisit the story as they discuss the vocabulary and ideas presented. The event referred to in Question 6 is the Tiananmen Massacre of June 4, 1989.

Question 10 helps guide students to examine the structure of the speech, in which the thesis statement is found at the end of paragraph 3: "...it is important to consider and reassess the position, rights and responsibilities of individuals, nations and peoples with respect to each other and to the planet as a whole."

In an essay or article, the thesis statement is usually found in the opening paragraph. However, because a speaker must gain the full attention and interest of his audience before introducing the main point, he often sets the stage with some brief introductory remarks.

DISCUSSION

The "hands-on" exercise in participatory democracy outlined in the first activity is designed to spark discussion and debate. Your academic institution may already have a policy outlining students' rights and responsibilities, whether this is stated explicitly, or included implicitly in the rules and regulations governing student behavior. This policy may form the basis for this discussion.

The balance of the questions are intended to encourage students to think about and discuss various issues relating to our rights and responsibilities as human beings. Because these issues are, in some cases, abstract, it may be helpful to relate the discussion to examples drawn from current political or economic events.

VOCABULARY BUILDING

Denotation and Connotation

Because this exercise involves abstract concepts, it may be quite difficult for students. You might find them saying, "Oh yes, I know what you mean...I just don't know how to say it."

As a result, it probably works best if it's completed in class, possibly in pairs or groups of three to start with, then as a discussion with the whole class. It may even be spread over several classes, with students tackling two or three pairs of words at a time. The sentences students suggest as examples will vary.

1. Love: A strong feeling of attachment, enthusiasm or devotion for someone, usually with whom we have a personal relationship.
   Admiration: A high regard for someone; delighted approval.
   Both words describe a strong positive feeling. However, we love someone for what he is—his inherent qualities—while we admire someone for what she does—her accomplishments.
2. Compassion: Sympathy for another's suffering, distress or unhappiness leading to a desire to alleviate it.
   Pity: Sympathetic sorrow for a someone who is suffering, distressed or unhappy.
   Both words describe sensitivity to another's pain. However, compassion connotes a move toward action whereas pity is simply a feeling.
3. Crime: An act that is forbidden by law.
   Sin: An act that is contrary to a religious or moral code.
   Both words describe wrongdoing; however, crime has a legal connotation, whereas sin has a moral or ethical connotation.
4. Responsibility: A state of being accountable for one's actions.
   Blame: A state of incurring disapproval or reproach as a result of one's actions.
   Although both words involve being answerable for our conduct, responsibility often has a neutral or even positive connotation, while blame has a negative connotation.

5. Happiness: A pleasurable state of well-being.
   Peace of mind: A state of mental or spiritual tranquillity.
   Both words denote contentment. However, happiness usually involves positive feelings generated by good fortune, while peace of mind connotes a state of overall serenity.
6. Sentient: Responsive to or conscious of sense impressions.
   Intelligent: Possessing the ability to reason, learn and understand.
   Both words describe a creature's consciousness of its environment. However, intelligence involves knowing and understanding, whereas sentience stops at awareness.
7. Respect: Feeling of high or special regard.
   Tolerance: Willingness to endure or permit something to exist without interference.
   While both words describe acceptance, tolerance, unlike respect, does not necessarily connote approval.
8. Sanctuary: A place of refuge and protection.
   Reservation: A place set aside for special use.
   Both words describe a place that is kept for a particular purpose. However, sanctuary implies that protection and care are offered. This is not the case with a reservation.
9. Nationalism: Loyalty to one nation above all others.
   Patriotism: Love for or devotion to one's country.
   Both words describe devotion to one's native land. However, nationalism suggests that a person considers her land superior to others. Patriotism does not.
10. Racism: Irrational hostility directed against an individual or group on the basis of their race.
    Prejudice: Irrational hostility directed toward an individual, group, race or their supposed characteristics.
    Both words denote hostility. While racism is based on race alone, prejudice may be based on a variety of factors including color, gender, mental or physical attributes, religion, age, etc.

WRITING

These essay topics require students to formulate an opinion and construct a logical argument to support it. Remind them to use concrete examples to develop their argument and substantiate their position.

GRAMMAR

Transitional Expressions

Because there may be more than one appropriate expression for each example, these are simply suggestions.

1. on the other hand
2. therefore
3. however
4. moreover
5. otherwise
6. nevertheless
7. undoubtedly
8. consequently
9. nonetheless
10. subsequently, later

Gerunds and Infinitives

Individual answers will vary. Here are some suggestions.
1. ...raising the awareness of the need to respect human rights and freedoms.
2. ...to consider what the Dalai Lama said in his address.
3. ...to pursue happiness and peace.
4. ...developing love and compassion for all sentient beings.
5. ...to demand equal rights and freedoms under the law.
6. ...to follow the path of peace.
7. ...by insisting that governments respect everyone equally.

FOLLOW-UP

1. Suggest that the class work up a proposal for a waste-management program to submit to the institution they're attending, together with a rationale developed along the lines outlined by the Dalai Lama.
2. As a group project, the class might select one environmental issue affecting the community, and write letters identifying the problem and offering solutions. These should include a rationale based on the principle of rights and responsibilities set out in the Dalai Lama's address.

UNIT 6

The Shape of the Law

PRE-READING

Invite the class to free-write on one of the following topics:

— Are there any circumstances under which it might be acceptable for a parent to take the life of a child?
— A civilized nation is judged by the way it treats its elderly and its children.

COMPREHENSION

In question 1, a "bogey" is a groundless fear that may, nevertheless, be used to influence people's opinion's of someone or something.

Questions 2 through 6 provide a framework for revisiting the story, preparing students for the discussion that follows. Questions 7 to 10 deal with the writing craft and are designed to raise students' awareness of Mowat's technique.

DISCUSSION

1. This question is designed to stimulate debate about whether morality is absolute or relative to particular circumstances.
2. The trial of the Ihalmiut mother provides an opportunity for students to restate Mowat's arguments, and develop their ability to adopt a position, argue a convincing case and spot flaws in their opponent's reasoning. Emphasize the importance of separating their personal opinion from the case they are making.
3. These expressions should prompt free-ranging discussion.

VOCABULARY BUILDING

Prefixes and Suffixes

1. a. pesticide
   b. insecticide
   c. suicide
   d. matricide
   e. patricide
   f. homicide
   g. genocide
2. a. disinherit
   b. irresponsible
   c. unwelcome
   d. impractical
   e. disagree
   f. unattractive
   g. irregular
   h. impure
   i. disbelief, unbelief
   j. unbearable
   k. abnormal
   l. uninteresting
   m. disallow
   n. immortal
   o. unimaginative
   p. discontinue
   q. asymmetrical
   r. disregard
   s. unlisted
   t. insane

WRITING

1. This topic requires students to choose a writing "voice," which may not represent their own—good practice in developing an awareness that there may be more than one side to a story.
2. The approach outlined in Unit 2 (see p. 25 of this guide) may help students organize this essay, which involves comparing and contrasting.

BEYOND THE CLASSROOM

In addition to providing practice in retelling a story, this survey may supply interesting information about people's opinions on the issues. These may become the basis for further debate.

GRAMMAR

Prepositions

Answers will vary.

Kinds of Sentences

It's sometimes helpful to illustrate sentence structure by drawing a diagram on the chalkboard to show the relationships among the people who live in a duplex.

Susan lives in the upper apartment. She has a job and is self-supporting; therefore, she is *independent*; this is analogous to a SIMPLE sentence.

The downstairs apartment is occupied by Marie and her six-month-old son. Marie is the *principal* member of the family and, though capable of surviving on her own, must look after her *dependent* child. This is analogous to a COMPLEX sentence.

Meanwhile, Susan is thinking of saving money by asking her cousin, Emily, to move in with her. Emily also works and is self-supporting. If they become roommates, each will still be *independent*; this is analogous to a COMPOUND sentence.

The entire duplex, with its two connected apartments, is analogous to a COMPOUND-COMPLEX sentence.

1. was forced: SIMPLE
2. did, was dictated: COMPLEX
3. walked, arrived: COMPOUND
4. knew, must go, could...carry: COMPLEX
5. left, could...take care, had...been weaned: COMPOUND-COMPLEX
6. did...know: SIMPLE
7. did...know, should do: COMPLEX
8. followed, had, live: COMPOUND-COMPLEX
9. walked: SIMPLE
10. is, judge, is, had: COMPOUND-COMPLEX

Reduction of Clauses to Phrases
1. There is a place in the great plains called the Lake of the Dead Child.
2. People living in the far North are often forced to make hard choices.
3. The man was unable to hunt because of his illness.
4. The food left by the woman was enough to keep her husband alive for two weeks.
5. You can still see the toys and other gifts brought by the parents to the grave of their dead child.

6. Women capable of bearing children are second in importance to their husbands.
   Women of child-bearing age are second in importance to their husbands.
7. Despite the blizzards, the woman managed to reach her family.
8. Nobody can possibly know the thoughts of the woman walking across the Barrens.
9. Upon reaching her kinsmen's igloos, she told them about her experience.
10. Each year of their lives, the woman and her husband returned to place gifts on the cairn marking the grave of their first-born.

FOLLOW-UP

The activities in Unit 21—A Living Will—complement this unit.

UNIT 7

The Wages of Sin

PRE-READING

Suggest that students free-write about the ideas and feelings generated by the photograph on page 78 of *Reflections*.

COMPREHENSION

1. This playfully irreverent misquote suggests that sin is rewarded rather than punished.
2. "Old wealth" is family wealth that has been handed down from one generation to the next. The narrator has only recently become rich, possibly by questionable means.
3. These descriptions engage the senses and, in one way or another, generate feelings of the kind of safety and security that comes from knowing that one's place in the world is assured.
4. The narrator seems to value old things that suggest good taste and economic status, along with comfort. The things he describes as drawbacks might be considered tacky in some circles. It seems he wants to acquire instant "class" along with his new-found wealth; he is something of a snob.
5. Driftwood refers to pieces of wood, often tree branches, that have floated in water before washing up on shore. The cottage is full of these pieces of "found art." Perhaps the tides of fortune or circumstances have shaped Onyx John and washed him up in this cottage to hide away like the driftwood.
6. This conversational, one-word sentence sums up Onyx John's emotional response to the entire situation—the house, its furnishings, its location, the view, everything. It also leads us to wonder "perfect for what?" Other examples of this device create snapshot images of the cottage or convey Onyx John's pride in his possessions in a conversational, telegraphic style.

43

7. This description is stereotypically macho. Onyx John invests ownership of this particular car with qualities he would like to possess: if the swiftest predator on earth, the cheetah, has been tamed and is at his beck and call, he must be powerful and masterful indeed!
8. In Onyx John's view, the disease is probably poverty.
9. They betray Onyx John's ambivalence about the superiority of his new lifestyle. At the same time as he supplies himself with both imported and upscale domestic beer, he comforts himself with a familiar brand, evoking "memories of home." He distinguishes between drinking beer because it is all he can afford, and being a true beer lover, even a connoisseur. If the former owners of his cottage can reveal the common touch—the cheap knick-knacks—he can "guzzle his brew" straight from the bottle.
10. "The Dish" probably refers to a woman. The capital letter and the fact that she is coming to take him sailing suggest a person.

DISCUSSION

In addition to examining the influence of advertising in defining our lifestyle choices, these questions and activities are designed to spark lively discussion about the stereotypical assumptions we sometimes make about money and socio-economic class.

Answers to the fourth question will vary.

VOCABULARY BUILDING

Denotation and Connotation

It may be appropriate to draw students' attention to the fact that English has the largest vocabulary of any major world language. Not only has English adopted many words from other languages, but it is also able to create new words very easily by changing inflections and manipulating word order.

Example   A very large bird with a yellow belly, which is sitting on a tree stump...
A great yellow-bellied stump-sitter...

This exercise, like the one in Unit 5, works well as a small-group activity. If each group is assigned two or three groups of words, the results of their discussion can be shared with the rest of the class.

Proverbs and Quotations

You might ask students to paraphrase the proverbs and quotations, give an example and share similar sayings from other cultures.

WRITING

The first of these assignments requires students to revisit the story, while the second calls for them to use their imaginations to come up with a plausible explanation. The third topic requires students to take a point of view and develop a convincing argument.

BEYOND THE CLASSROOM

This is a good opportunity to encourage students to prepare brief oral presentations on the topics they have chosen.

GRAMMAR

Conditional: Present Hypothetical

Answers will vary.

Using the Conditional

Both exercises provide students with opportunities to practise transferring grammar theory to authentic writing and to edit their own work. The first requires them to use the hypothetical conditional construction, while the second involves the past unreal conditional.

Prepositions of Place

1. in, on, on (near, beside), near (next to), in (of)
2. of, in, outside, in, from, through (into), on
3. by (near, at), for, in, beside, on
4. in, in, out of (from), into, to, along (across), of, up, of
5. to, on, along (up, down), on (onto), at, of, in, along, in

FOLLOW-UP

Brainteasers

Photocopy the following page and invite students to work individually, in pairs or in groups to solve these word puzzles, many of which involve prepositions. To help get them started, copy the examples shown here onto the chalkboard and solve them together.

<p align="center">S s H in O g i W n E g R
(<i>Singing in the shower</i>)</p>

<p align="center">C O O K E D
bit
(<i>A bit undercooked</i>)</p>

Answers

Column 1
Dionne quintuplets
Split second
Icebox
Day after day <i>or</i> day by day
To be overconfident
A bit underdone
A bird in the hand is worth two in the bush
Just between friends
Yesterday afternoon
Klingon warrior (from <i>Star Trek</i>)

Column 2
Abuse (U's)
Strong undertow
Just in time
Serial (cereal) killer
My in-laws
Drug overdose
Difficult to foresee
I'm beside myself
Once (ones) in a while
Ring around the collar

Column 3
Low income
Age before beauty
Apple pie (pi)
A little misunderstanding
Look backwards <i>or</i> a backward look
Easy on the eyes (I's)
Step backwards <i>or</i> a backward step
I'll see you around sometime
Safety in numbers
A lovers' triangle

D ――― *babybabybabybabybaby*	ABUUUUU	COLOWME
SEC OND	TOE STRONG	AGEB4BEAUTY
I C E C C E C I	**TjIusMtE**	A PULL 3.14159265
DAYDAY	*Cheerios/Wheaties/ Corn Flakes/Muslix/ Shreddies/ Grape Nuts/ All Bran* *KILLER*	**STANDING** miss
2B CONFIDENT	**LAMYWS**	KOOL
DONE bit	Drug Dose	EASY ――― **I I I I I I**
TaHEbHiArNdD = THtEBwUSoH	DIFFICULT 2 4 C	PETS

FRIEND
 	
JUST
 	
FRIEND
	I'M/MYSELF	l
		  l s
		' e
		I sometime e
		  u y
		    o

NOONYESTERDAY	**AWoneoneoneHILE**	63S5A78F21E99T578Y371
CLING WARRIOR	(COLLAR)	L O V E R O E V V E O R L A

UNIT 8
The Avalon Notes

PRE-READING

Challenge students to incorporate these five words into a brief narrative: ocean, child, red, alone, dog.
    This can be an individual free-writing or oral group activity.

COMPREHENSION

Students' responses to questions 1 and 2 will vary.

3. This sentence often causes perplexity. Because the author never reveals the reason, readers are left to use their imaginations.
4. While Brown appeals directly to our sense of sight and touch (e.g., "the sand is salmon pink"), she appeals indirectly to our sense of hearing. As we are caught up in the scene, we probably "hear" the dog barking and the children laughing and shouting in our imaginations.
5. In a painting, an artist may enhance, diminish or even alter the components of a scene according to his interpretation of what is actually there; a photographer is obliged to work with the scene as it really is, though she can offer a personal perspective by adjusting lighting, camera angles and so on. Both "painting" and "photograph" suggest a filtered view of reality. The woman feels filtered out of reality, as if she is a spectator rather than a participant in the activity at the beach.
6. Opinions are likely to vary considerably. Some students may suggest that she was weak from an illness. Others may think that she has recently suffered a loss—the death of a parent or lover, or a divorce—that has caused her to withdraw from society. Still others may say that she intended to commit suicide but has decided against it, and plans to build up her strength by taking a twice-daily walk.

7. The use of the present tense suggests a timelessness to the piece. We are drawn more immediately into the scene, and begin to add details of our own. See the introductory remarks to discussion activity 2 on page 88-89 of *Reflections*.

DISCUSSION

These questions are designed to extend some of the issues raised in earlier discussions and help students develop their awareness of the symbolic and spiritual overtones of this piece, enabling them to make "The Avalon Notes" their own.

VOCABULARY BUILDING

These sayings were selected to help broaden students' knowledge of common idioms.

WRITING

Both these activities encourage students to use their imaginations to fill in details.

GRAMMAR

Prepositions
1. across (through, into), over
2. up (along), of, near (above, at)
3. along (on), by (beside)
4. to (into), in, on (at)
5. to, at, of
6. into, near
7. through, to (into)

Ten Years with the Same Dog

PRE-READING

A DRTA (see p. 9) can be used to introduce this reading. Or, invite students to free-write on this topic: If you could spend one week as an animal, which would you choose to be and why?

COMPREHENSION

1. Working implies doing something that may or may not involve payment; earning a living implies that a living wage is received for work done. For example, housework or volunteer work is "work" but does not earn one a living.
2. Start by asking the class what images these places conjure up for them. For Brown in Australia, these European destinations might be synonymous with art and culture. It may be interesting to ask why she chooses Spain and Paris, rather than Spain and France, and what students think she hopes to find there.
3. "Once" suggests that Brown tried golf—and never wishes to repeat the experience. Unlike golf, most of the other sports she mentions are fast and active. Even fishing, especially deep-sea fishing, has moments of high drama to offset the hours of waiting. Most of the games she plays are competitive, involving skill and intelligence. Her inclusion of *Space Invaders* suggests a willingness to try new things. She seems to be an active, outgoing, passionate person who enjoys a challenge.
4. Some students may suggest that this sentence reveals a certain carelessness about time. Brown may have become so involved in what she was doing that she forgot to wind her clock or to put the sugar back into its container to keep it soft. Others may

interpret it to mean that she has spent time in her life waiting—long enough for the clock to stop and the sugar to go hard.
5. She seems to care deeply for the dog. Indeed, she appears to have had a longer relationship with her dog than with any human being. Her feelings of responsibility toward the dog are strong enough to keep her from doing what she wants.
6. Brown uses the present perfect to indicate indefinite time in the past. She is not providing us with a chronology of her life's activities; she is merely listing them.
7. Answers will vary.
8. The title is somewhat humorous. We are more accustomed to hearing this about people—"I've been with (living with, married to) the same person for 10 years"—than animals. In addition, the title suggests a relationship with, rather than ownership of, the dog. Brown could have said, "I've *had* the same dog for 10 years," rather than "I've *been with*..."

DISCUSSION

The first question usually sparks lively debate, particularly among immigrants who must often take jobs that are at odds with their education and experience. Answers to the other questions will vary. When discussing the third question, you might mention that cats are the number 1 pet choice in North America, and discuss the reasons.

VOCABULARY

1. dwellings, residences
2. sports
3. games
4. card games
5. vehicles, modes of transport
6. bodies of water
7. philosophical movements
8. Asian methods of achieving physical and mental health
9. pets
10. esoteric systems of divination

WRITING

1. This activity co-ordinates well with discussion question 5.

2. This short essay provides practice in developing a thesis and a logical argument to support it. It might be useful to remind students to back up their points with concrete examples.
3. Composing this letter provides practice in transactional writing; that is, presenting a case to a known audience for a particular purpose (see also writing topic 2, Unit 4, p. 33 of this guide).
4. This short essay provides practice in developing a thesis.

GRAMMAR

Verb Tenses

These exercises offer students an opportunity to practise using the present perfect tense.

Verb Tenses—Description versus Action

The first activity stresses use of the simple present tense, while the second stresses the simple past.

Sentence Combining—Complex Sentences

1. We lived in the suburbs when I was a child.
2. Louis has been living in New York since 1991.
3. Henry came to work today although he has the flu.
4. The little boy ate too much cake because he was greedy.
   Note: Students often display fuzzy logic by misplacing "because" and saying, "Because the little boy ate too much cake, he was greedy."
5. By the time (that) we reached the veterinary hospital, the dog had died.
   Note: It may be necessary to explain the use of the past perfect tense here.
6. I sprained my ankle last week while I was playing golf.
   Note: We would usually say, "I sprained my ankle last week while playing golf."
7. I might have to wait until the dog dies to get to Spain and Paris.

UNIT 9

My Private Solitude

PRE-READING

Is there a difference between learning a second language and learning a foreign language? Students might discuss this question in small groups, or free-write about it.

COMPREHENSION

1. By calling French a "foreign tongue," even though it's one of Canada's official languages, MacIntosh emphasizes how strange and unknown it was to her.
2. MacIntosh's teacher tortured students by yelling at them whenever they made a mistake. The words "wounds" and "scar tissue" continue the metaphor.
3. The francophones were far richer than MacIntosh and her peers because they were bilingual, speaking excellent English, while she and her friends were unilingual.
4. She believed her neighbors robbed her of money by doing jobs she should have been allowed to do. MacIntosh's mother hired a francophone boy to do Saturday chores, and gave the job of milking their cow to his mother in exchange for half the milk.
5. All are military words suggesting war. MacIntosh sees her attempts to learn French as a kind of battle. In Paragraph 8 she says, "I would *attack* and *conquer* this impossible language." In Paragraph 11, she says, "...I could *confront* this language, *mount a frontal attack*, and emerge *victorious*."
6. She felt intimidated because the French skills of the other students seemed more proficient than hers. The fact that many spoke languages besides English and French added to her feelings of inadequacy. You might ask students whether they think MacIntosh's French is as poor as she seems to think.

7. The professor used his position to introduce a historical and political element to his classes, stereotyping MacIntosh and blaming her and her family for the fact that francophones were not as well off economically as English Quebecers.
8. The symbols she describes are from the international phonetic alphabet.
9. Her belief that listening to her classmates' answers was wrong prevented her from cheating. Referring to this as espionage continues the military metaphor.
10. General James Wolfe was a British soldier who defeated the French General Montcalm in the Battle of the Plains of Abraham in 1759, winning Canada for the British. Both Wolfe and Montcalm were killed in the battle.

DISCUSSION

The first two questions provide an excellent opportunity for students to examine and discuss effective teaching and learning techniques, while the third promotes their understanding of the differences among languages. The fourth encourages them to return to the story and practise making inferences.

VOCABULARY BUILDING

Decoding Idioms
Guide the students through a discussion of the meaning of these idioms. Composing a sentence using each is an exercise that can be completed individually in writing or as a written or oral group activity. Answers will vary.

Synonyms
1. rhythm
2. metamorphosis
3. surreptitiously
4. disquieting
5. thrifty
6. appointed
7. overcome
8. remnants
9. reticent
10. amenable

WRITING

The first activity offers students an opportunity to express themselves freely while requiring them to develop their own structure. The second is an integrated project that draws on a number of skills, including the ability to work in a group. For the third, which requires students to compare, you may wish to use the preparation techniques outlined on page 25 of this guide.

GRAMMAR

Verbs: Conditional (Unreal)

This exercise provides students with an opportunity to transfer what they have learned about grammar theory to authentic writing.

Sentence Combining—Subordinate Clauses

While answers will vary, ensure that students complete the exercise according to instructions. You may wish to extend this exercise by pointing out that creating subordinate clauses is not the only method of subordination. Suggestions for the first question are provided.

1. I was interested only in getting a decent mark that would satisfy my parents' ambitions for me.
   Alternatives
   I was only interested in getting a decent mark to satisfy my parents' ambitions.
   My only interest in getting a decent mark was to satisfy my parents' ambitions.

FOLLOW-UP

Invite groups of students to design five to seven questions for a survey of people's feelings about learning a second (or third) language. They can then collect responses from a range of language learners—someone who speaks their own language, a native speaker of English, someone who is bilingual (English and ...), a child, a grandparent and so on. Encourage them to include both female and male respondents.

UNIT 10

The Stepmother

PRE-READING

The stereotypical images that may be evoked by the title—and carried through in the first few paragraphs—make a DRTA (see p. 9) an excellent strategy for introducing this reading.

Alternatively, encourage students to brainstorm to come up with a list of compound nouns containing the word "mother." Discuss the connotations of each (e.g., stepmother, mother-in-law, grandmother, etc.) and what this indicates about our concept of "mother."

COMPREHENSION

1. Discuss our images of the stereotypical "wicked stepmother"—and how this is changing as a result of a changing definition of "family" in today's society where divorce is more common.
2. The use of the subjunctive suggests that the narrator believes the opposite—that it was Fatima's fault, and she really didn't care. The description suggests that Fatima truly has been grieving.
3. The narrator and her mother believe that Fatima is responsible for Savo Djon's painful death. The narrator is so outraged that she doesn't want to offer Fatima their condolences.
4. The author's first impression of Fatima was of a kind, generous and gracious woman, one of the few people willing to shelter refugees. She offered them wonderful food, and paid attention to the little girl, to whom she seemed like a mysterious queen.
5. Savo Djon was thin, tired and sad-looking while Alua was chubby, pretty and healthy-looking. Savo Djon wore plain, dark clothes and went only to the square, while Alua wore beautiful dresses and accompanied her mother on outings. Alua went to school, but Savo Djon worked. Savo Djon even ate apart from the others, and did her own cooking. The evidence seemed to indicate that Fatima favored her own child over her stepdaughter.

6. The legend teaches us that appearances may be deceiving. Just as the people of Samarkand misjudged the princess's gift, so the child misjudged Fatima for treating her daughters so differently.
7. The author hoped Savo Djon would identify with Cinderella and rebel against Fatima. However, Savo Djon felt sorry for the stepmother and stepsisters because they were so unhappy. This reveals that she thinks things through logically, and has a forgiving, compassionate, non-judgmental nature.
8. In a community such as this, gossip is a major pastime. As a result, keeping Savo Djon's leprosy a secret was more difficult. Fatima made no attempt to explain her apparent preference for Alua, allowing her neighbors to draw their own conclusions.
9. She probably hoped she would not be judged harshly by people to whom she had extended nothing but kindness and generosity. Her sense of personal dignity may have contributed to her reluctance to explain herself.
10. Her majesty is manifest in her dignified and discreet behavior. She did not feel compelled to explain her actions; she placed her love for her stepdaughter above obedience to the law and seemed almost untouched by public opinion.

DISCUSSION

"The Stepmother" raises a number of issues that can spark lively discussion: whether a birth mother's love is superior to a foster mother's; society's discomfort with serious illness and disfigurement; whether children's stories shape—or reflect—society's attitudes; the components of racial discrimination; the extent to which we censor facts that don't fit our preconceived notions; the legal right of parents to administer physical punishment; the mercy killing debate; and the historical context in which all these issues arise.

Students sometimes judge Fatima harshly. This is an opportunity to discuss how attitudes toward parenting differ from culture to culture and from the past to the present.

It's interesting to compare Fatima's action with that of Robert Latimer, the Alberta farmer who, in 1994, was found guilty of murdering his 12-year-old daughter, a victim of a painful form of cerebral palsy. Be on the lookout for other contemporary real-life stories involving mercy killing to update the discussion.

VOCABULARY BUILDING

Synonyms
1. adamant
2. huddled
3. amulet
4. betrothed
5. ferocious
6. ajar
7. pondered
8. squatted
9. scolded
10. pouch
11. veranda
12. dishevelled
13. cease
14. cavity
15. enlightenment
16. colony
17. fatigued
18. penalty
19. bewildered
20. erect

Figurative Language
1. Guide students by directing them to one or two specific passages. For example, on page 109, they will find the similes, "…like a miracle," and "…like a mysterious queen."
2. Answers will vary.

WRITING

These activities help students understand that so-called empirical evidence may lead to more than one conclusion. The first calls on them to compare interpretations, while the second asks them to create a subjective account of events. The third involves evaluating actions, drawing inferences and supporting them with examples, while the fourth challenges them to develop a clearly stated thesis.

GRAMMAR

Though students' responses may vary somewhat, it's important to stress the correct use of the subjunctive and the conditional.

Verbs: Subjunctive Describing Situations That Resemble Reality
1. The child covered his face with his hands as though he were crying.
2. The gentleman dressed as though he were wealthy.
3. The little girl ate greedily, as though she were starving.

4. Mabel treats Henry as though she loved him.
5. Because of the damaged door, the house looked as though it had been robbed.
6. The soup tasted as though it had been burned.
7. Fatima was crying and wailing as if she really cared.
8. The dishes didn't look as though they had been washed.
9. Emily is spending money as though she were a millionaire.
10. Your house looks as though it has been freshly painted.

Verbs: The Conditional—Present Conditional and Past Unreal
1. Fatima told Savo Djon that if she beat her until she bled, the police would not want to touch her.
2. If Savo Djon had not gone to work selling pittas in the square, her leprosy might have been discovered at school.
3. If Savo Djon understood the similarities between her own life and Cinderella's, she would think that Fatima was a cruel stepmother.
4. The doctors had told Fatima that leprosy was not as contagious as people thought if Savo Djon kept clean and used certain spices and herbs in cooking.
5. If the pitta buyer had not worked with lepers, she would not have recognized Savo Djon's disease.
6. Madame Solomonovna would never have understood Fatima's actions if Fatima had not explained them to her.
7. If Fatima were not Savo Djon's stepmother, perhaps people would not suspect her of killing the child.

Writing Effective Topic Sentences
Answers will vary.

FOLLOW-UP

Select a familiar children's story, such as *Cinderella*, and invite the class to work in groups to retell it from the point of view of one of the other characters—one of the stepsisters, for example—in a way that avoids stereotypes. Students might, for example, create an extremely retiring Cinderella, who is too shy to go to the ball despite her sisters' encouragement.

UNIT 11

The Essay

Family Silliness, Domestic Clowning

PRE-READING

In the personal or familiar essay, the writer draws readers' attention to an ordinary object, event or experience. He or she then explores its significance, revealing some deeper truth that both writer and reader can share.

As an oral or free-writing activity, encourage students to describe a special occasion when their entire family had dinner together.

COMPREHENSION

These questions are designed to encourage students to reflect upon their own experiences of family gatherings. Many of the words singled out here are abstract and often pose difficulty for second-language learners.

1. The jokes may not seem funny—or even appropriate—outside the context of a particular family. They are of the I-guess-you-had-to-be-there variety.
2. The dynamic of a fairly large group of people, all of whom share common experiences, sets off contagious laughter. The object of the humor may not be particularly funny in itself, but the shared sense of absurdity triggers laughter.
3. This question may lead to a discussion of humor, and how it is perceived differently from culture to culture.
4. This question underscores the importance of prepositions, which many students consider mere function words that are "empty" of meaning. "In it" means "being present and surrounded by" the family, while "of it" means "belonging to" the family.

5. This is an opportunity to introduce expressions such as "blood is thicker than water."
6. Like question 3, this may lead to a discussion of the fact that distinctions between comedy and slapstick vary among cultures.
7. Other words conveying a lack of dignity include "roaring," "screaming," "rowdy," "monkey business," "screeching" and "bellowing." Note that many of these words are verbs.
8. These occasions may be important because their memories evoke love and a sense of belonging.

DISCUSSION

1. Depending on their cultural background, students may have different experiences of family life. You might extend this question by asking them about the role language plays in their family gatherings. For example, an Italian family may speak Italian at gatherings because the grandparents cannot speak English; but the children may speak English together, partly so that their elders can't understand them. Priestley's scenario presupposes a unilingual family situation.
2. This question asks students to think beyond the essay. You might introduce the saying, "Friends are the family you choose."
3. This question draws upon students' previous knowledge, requiring them to transfer skills of observation and analysis across languages and, possibly, cultures.

VOCABULARY BUILDING

Antonyms
1. domestic
2. roaring
3. sensitive
4. outsider
5. delight
6. repulsive
7. rowdy
8. collective
9. ebbing
10. regret

Popular Sayings
These expressions enable the students to discuss various attitudes towards humor and the expression of emotion.

WRITING

The first task invites students to share a family event with the reader in a personal way, while the second calls for them to develop a clearly stated thesis.

GRAMMAR

Sentence Combining—Verbal Phrases

While the precise wording of students' answers may vary, it is important to emphasize the correct use of verbal phrases.

1. After preparing an end-of-summer barbecue for 14, Louise and I decided to invite the entire family.
2. We charcoal-broiled a dozen steaks ordered specially from the market by my sister-in-law.
3. Everyone of us was in the right mood to enjoy the festivities.
4. Playing Frisbee with the kids seemed to be the excuse I needed to romp about on the grass.
5. Leaping high into the air, my dog caught the Frisbee almost as many times as I did.
6. Wagging her tail happily, she returned the Frisbee to the person who had thrown it.
7. We have decided that it is important to make this end-of-summer barbecue an annual event.

On Hope and Suicide

PRE-READING

This rather difficult piece on hope goes far beyond the dictionary definition to a more philosophical discussion of the abstract concept. Havel's reflections can form the basis of a discussion about extended definitions and levels of meaning, and about how a common word such as hope can be used in a number of different ways, some of them simple and some profound.

Write the words "hope" and "suicide" on the chalkboard and invite students to free-write about the thoughts they evoke.

COMPREHENSION

1. Hope is an inner belief, rather than a logical assessment of how things are likely to turn out.
2. Hope is an ability to work toward something because it is good in itself, regardless of the outcome. Optimism anticipates the best possible outcome for a situation. Hope is centred on the process, not on the outcome.
3. This question enables students to see how well they have understood Havel's meaning. Draw their attention to the fact that Havel himself restates his idea several different ways.
4. Answers will vary depending on what is happening at the time, and students' experience and backgrounds.
5. Havel compares suicide to a rope stretched above him that he can grab whenever he doesn't have the strength to go on.
6. He will probably not kill himself precisely because the possibility of suicide exists.
7. Introduce the idea of paradox by citing examples of statements that may seem contradictory (e.g., It is important not to skip meals when you are on a diet). Havel says that thinking about the fact that suicide will end the joys as well as the pain of life gives him the strength to face living.
8. Nobody can possibly know how much pain another person is experiencing, or decide for another when this pain has become too great to bear.
9. Helping someone find the will to live is the most important element in persuading him or her not to commit suicide.
10. According to Havel, people who kill themselves place a very high value on life, refusing to live it when it falls short of their expectations. By showing us the point at which life is no longer viable, they show us the real meaning of life.

DISCUSSION

These questions are designed to encourage students to form and express their own opinions about the ideas presented in this—and other—essays.

VOCABULARY BUILDING

Prefixes and Suffixes

Students' responses will vary.

WRITING

Both writing tasks are creative and personal.

GRAMMAR

Verbs—Indirect Speech

Encourage students to pay close attention to the tense of the verb used to report what was said. In questions 2 and 6, for example, the present tense—"that hope *is*...," "whether life *isn't*..."—is preferable because it indicates a continuing belief, rather than something that took place in the past and is now finished.

1. The writer asked whether Havel saw a grain of hope anywhere in the 1980s.
2. Havel said that hope is definitely not the same thing as optimism.
3. The author asked Havel if he thought suicide was a solution.
4. Havel said (that) he had never yet attempted suicide, and it didn't seem likely that he would try it in the near future.
5. Havel wondered if there was anyone who had never thought of suicide.
6. Havel asked whether life isn't a kind of permanent deferral of suicide until later.
7. Havel said (that) the arguments he'd used on such occasions would probably not have persuaded him if he'd been on the other end of them.
8. Havel asked whether we have any right at all to take such a high and mighty attitude to something we haven't known.
9. He said (that) he couldn't answer the question about whether suicide is a solution or not.
10. The warden ordered Havel not to interfere in the running of his camp.

PROOFREADING AND EDITING

1. Everyone in the family contributes by telling stories and making jokes.
2. I gave the airline bag that I usually stow in the overhead luggage compartment to the flight attendant.
   I gave the flight attendant the airline bag that I usually stow in the overhead luggage compartment.
3. Although George's allergies are not as severe as last year, he is unable to play baseball.
4. I drove a car when I was young, but I prefer taking public transportation nowadays.
5. Last night, I was watching the hockey game on TV when you telephoned me.
   Note: "Last night" can also be placed after "TV" or at the end of the sentence.
6. The local TV station that I usually watch has less information about world soccer scores than the cable sports station.
7. The doctor prescribed Aspirin and plenty of rest because George's mother had the flu.
8. If Vinoy gets his promotion, he will be able to visit his family back home.
9. Last month, Emily visited the town she grew up in.
   Last month, Emily visited the town where she grew up.
10. He told us that he was so hungry that he could have (could've) eaten two dinners.

FOLLOW-UP

Students may appreciate a complete change of pace from this rather sombre piece of writing. The following riddles are fun and can be used whenever a bit of a break is needed.

Riddle 1

Farmer Brown decides to visit his new neighbors across the river. He takes his dog, Rover, with him for protection, a sack of carrots as a gift for his neighbors, and a rabbit as a pet for their little girl. When he comes to the river, he realizes that he has a problem. His boat is very small—so small, in fact, that it can carry only him and either the dog or the carrots or the rabbit.

Farmer Brown can't leave the dog on either bank with the rabbit because the dog will eat the rabbit. Similarly, he can't leave the rabbit with the carrots because the rabbit just loves to eat carrots! How can Farmer Brown safely transport everything to the other side of the river?

First, Farmer Brown takes the rabbit across the river and returns. Then, he takes the carrots across and brings the rabbit back with him. He leaves the rabbit behind and transports the dog across. Now the dog and the carrots are on the other side of the river. Finally, he returns to his own side and transports the rabbit across.

Riddle 2

George has been invited to visit an old friend at his cabin deep in the woods. It has been several years since George visited his friend, and the landscape now looks quite different. George does fine until he comes to the final fork in the road. He knows one road leads to his friend's cabin and the other runs into a lake, but he can't remember which is which. Night is falling and he's anxious to get there. He decides to ask directions from the three brothers who live in a shack near the junction. However, George's friend has warned him about the brothers: two of them are always truthful, but the third always lies. George doesn't know which is the liar.

At the shack, George finds the brothers (we'll call them A, B and C) eager to help. He asks A: "Are you truthful, or are you a liar?" A mumbles something that George isn't able to hear. George asks B what A said. B replies, "A said he's a liar." George asks C what A said. C replies, "A said he always tells the truth."

Which brother does George ask for directions, and why?

Note: Make this riddle even more challenging by inviting the students to come up with the questions George needs to ask in order to obtain accurate directions.

George asks either A or C for directions. A must have said, "I tell the truth." (If A is truthful, he will say, "I tell the truth." If A is a liar, he will also say, "I tell the truth.") Because B said that A was a liar, B must be the liar. Therefore, A and C are truthful and will give George accurate directions.

UNIT 12

Poetry

Poetry can be used to accomplish a number of objectives in ESL classrooms. For example, a poem with a well-defined rhyme scheme can help students develop a feel for the rhythms of English, especially if it's read aloud, either individually or chorally. Most of the poems in this unit are short, lending themselves to detailed, close study. Because poetry often uses visual symbols—color, shape, sound and the unusual juxtaposition of images—to appeal to the emotions, students may "understand" a poem instinctively, then reach for the language to translate this perception into English. The extent to which you use poetry will depend on the students' interests and abilities.

The Road Not Taken

PRE-READING

Invite students to close their eyes and think about the place they would most like to be right now. Then, ask them to jot down words and phrases that describe the feeling created by the place. On a separate sheet of paper, ask them to jot down as many images as they can. Suggest that they exchange their image lists with a partner. Do the images evoke the same feelings for both students?

COMPREHENSION

1. It is autumn; the leaves are yellow.
2. The undergrowth may have obscured the path or there may be a small hill, making the road appear to bend.
3. This question involves a simple paraphrasing of the poem.
4. In keeping one road for another day, Frost displayed the optimism of youth. At the same time, however, he was experienced enough to know that he might never see this particular fork again.

5. This question offers students an opportunity to sharpen their appreciation of precise word choice.
6. Extend this discussion by relating the following true story.

    Though the wife of a Czech film-maker spoke little English, she often accompanied her husband to social functions, at which she gained a reputation as a sympathetic listener. Her secret? "Reading" the speaker's intonation to assess the emotional context and responding with "oh" in an appropriate tone.

    Invite the class to respond to a variety of utterances by simply varying the intonation of "oh."
7. His choice of road has made all the difference to the rest of his life.

DISCUSSION

1. This open-ended question enables students to relate Frost's ideas to their own experience of life.
2. The discipline of this rhyme scheme may have helped Frost focus his ideas and feelings. Using a traditional English sound pattern—the four-stress line of Anglo-Saxon metre—may suit Frost well in evoking an emotional connection in his readers.
3. Students may enjoy working in groups to create a rhythmic nursery rhyme, rap song or TV commercial to "perform" for the class.

WRITING

Most students have no difficulty coming up with an experience to write about. For the second assignment, you may wish to suggest some common rituals, such as getting ready for school.

Aftermath

PRE-READING

Ask students what their favorite season is and why. A lively discussion may develop as they consider the symbolic associations connected with the seasons, especially if the class includes students who come from countries where the seasons are quite different—e.g., where there are dry and monsoon seasons.

COMPREHENSION

1. The day is grey and heavy; she is depressed and troubled. It is fall, the season of discontinuation. She may be experiencing an ending of some kind.
2. We hear the pitter-patter of the rain, the crackle of the fire, the thump of the bird's tiny body on the glass—possibly, by extrapolation, the wind.
3. This is another opportunity for students to sharpen their appreciation of word choice.
4. The sparrow was physically injured, while the woman appears to be suffering emotional pain.
5. Attracted to the warmth and security of the fire, the bird was stopped by the glass window, an unseen barrier. We don't know what "fire" the woman was trying to reach, but something or someone blocked her path, too.
6. She has understood that the hurt can be healed, given a period of withdrawal, warmth and rest.
7. The adjective "trusting" describes the bird; the adverb "trustingly," however, describes only how the bird will fly.

DISCUSSION

1. Opinions will vary.
2. Revisit question 1 on page 143 of *Reflections*, which describes the levels on which poetry can be interpreted. Students may have some interesting ideas about what distinguishes art from mere writing. For example, they may suggest that if a poem does not involve a universal human experience, it isn't art.

WRITING

This is an opportunity for students to use their imaginations.

FOLLOW-UP

It is useful to demonstrate that poetry is often an attempt to communicate with readers at levels that are not always conscious. The poet may use abstract images, symbols, sound and even shape to communicate a feeling or concept.

One way of approaching images in poetry is to invite students to close their eyes and think of a feeling. Then, ask them to draw the feeling without using words. When they've finished, ask volunteers to display their creations. Encourage other students to guess what feeling is portrayed. They may find that the words come more easily once they've articulated the feelings non-verbally.

Extend this activity by inviting students to draw something like their city in rush hour or studying for final exams, etc. This time, they may not draw any recognizable people, places or things—simply abstract designs.

The Shark

PRE-READING

Brainstorm to make a list of words and phrases that describe sharks.

COMPREHENSION

1. The line signals danger. It indicates that the shark has come the harbor before, probably to hunt.
2. This question is designed to encourage discussion. You might refer to recent documentaries that show that sharks are not as dangerous to humans as the movies would have us believe.
3. This question focuses on Pratt's use of precise vocabulary.
4. The fact that nothing has changed enhances the lack of emotion in the shark. It seems untouched by the encounter.
5. Students will likely suggest a feeling of relief.
6. The vulture is a scavenger, while the wolf is a predator. The shark is both scavenger and predator.
7. This line underscores how alien the shark is.

DISCUSSION

Both these questions are designed to encourage wide-ranging, open-ended discussion.

WRITING

This assignment may bring out some interesting cultural variations.

FOLLOW-UP

Students might enjoy writing their own free verse about a wild creature about which they have strong feelings, positive or negative.

To My Son

PRE-READING

A DRTA (see p. 9) can be used to introduce this poem.
Note: This is perhaps the most challenging of the poems. It will require a fair degree of reflective, close reading.

COMPREHENSION

1. The sports described are skiing, skating and soccer.
2. The lines in the snow look like elongated I's. Perhaps he is asserting his unique personality through this individual sport. The words "assertive," "*your* messages," "*your* summer *declarations*" echo the pronoun.
3. The words are aggressive, impulsive, possibly even violent. They suggest that the boy feels a need to express himself and leave his mark—literally. The soccer shoe is "broken"—as a result of playing too hard? The glove and ball are "muddied"—he plays in all weathers, disregarding personal comfort; he shovels snow violently, "gouging" at winter; and the storm's "rage."
4. See answer 2. The boy might be trying to communicate his individuality to himself, his mother, and the world at large. Students may identify with Davis's son and add details from their own experience of growing up. Ask them what messages a daughter might leave.
5. Refer to answer 2.

Answers to questions 6 and 7 will vary.

DISCUSSION

These questions form the basis of a guided discussion of free-verse poetry. The "double exposure" technique outlined in question 2 is particularly effective with this poem.

As an extra task, invite students to imagine how the content of a poem titled "To My Daughter" might be different. Some students may argue that there won't be a difference—and away you go!

WRITING

This strategy can be applied effectively to a variety of writing tasks.

from Tao Teh Ching

PRE-READING

Invite students to form groups and decide on the world leader (living or dead) they would most like to meet. Then, brainstorm to identify what makes a good leader. Record the qualities on the chalkboard and save them for a follow-up discussion.

COMPREHENSION

1. A leader is usually thought of as someone who stands out from the crowd, guiding and directing the actions of others. It seems contradictory for a leader to be barely known; how would we know whom to follow?
2. Discuss the connotations of "acclaim" and "obey." For instance, "acclaim" suggests enthusiastic approval or lack of opposition, while "obey" suggests doing what another says without question. Both are dangerous because they imply the surrender of critical thinking.
3. This is more obviously true, because we can probably all agree that a leader we despise is a poor guide.
4. Students may refer to various versions of the golden rule, the Biblical teaching that we ought to behave toward others as we expect them to behave toward us.

5. Lao Tzu's good leader respects others, doesn't talk much, and guides people's actions indirectly.
6. These words suggest that Lao Tzu's leader has mastered the art of inhabiting the background rather than the limelight.
7. Answers will vary.

DISCUSSION

1. The process of understanding this poem leads us to its meaning. We come to understand it because we must invest energy in decoding it. This is a good opportunity to introduce the Asian belief that emphasizes process rather than outcome, the idea that "the way to do is to be."
2. This is an open-ended discussion question.

WRITING

1. This task, which requires students to illustrate their views with concrete examples, can also be a small-group discussion topic. It may be interesting to find out how students perceive power in these everyday relationships.
2. This creative exercise enables students to weave seemingly unrelated images into a coherent narrative or evocative description.
   This, too, can be an oral exercise. Form two teams of five and give them 10 minutes to prepare the "stories." The rest of the class can choose the best. Vary this activity by inviting each team to list five elements for another team to weave into a story.

VOCABULARY BUILDING

Two-Word Adjectives
1. George loves home-baked apple pie.
2. Emily sells handmade doll's clothes.
3. We can take a tour of the city in a horse-drawn carriage.
4. These computer-generated answers are correct.
5. I like soft-boiled eggs.
6. University-educated nursing students sometimes lack clinical experience.

7. George makes caramel-coated popcorn.
8. The AIDS-infected child was refused day-care facilities.
9. We sailed across the sun-sparkled waters of the lake.
10. I bought a new fur-lined jacket yesterday.

Figurative Language
Answers will vary.

GRAMMAR

Verb Tenses

1. are
2. would have answered
3. had asked
4. seemed
5. knows
6. read
7. was
8. thought
9. was
10. informed
11. was (really) talking
12. was
13. decided
14. was
15. suggested
16. accompany
17. are joking
18. is
19. trust
20. said
21. arrived
22. was
23. has gone
24. grumbled
25. began
26. forgot
27. gave
28. had
29. read
30. could
31. was describing (described)
32. had experienced
33. did (not) seem
34. could (not) imagine
35. could have expressed
36. says
37. can(not) be said
38. offered
39. would have laughed
40. is

Sentence Combining

The following is only one suggestion for completing this exercise, which will have many variations. This is an opportunity to point out the need to eliminate redundancy; for example, we don't need to add the word "car" if we say "convertible."

Although it is unseasonably chilly, it would be pleasant to go sailing on Lake Champlain next weekend, weather permitting. We could have a picnic lunch of bread, cheese, fruit and California wine purchased at a liquor store south of the border. We might take my convertible, if you're not afraid to drive with the top down.

Ynne Auncient Daeyes

Decoding the English in this poem may spark interest in the history of the language. Point out the thorn (þ), which has evolved into our "th." In the late medieval period, it was often written as y—the reason we sometimes see shops named Ye (The) Olde Curiosity Shoppe. Students are often surprised to learn that no academy rules on English usage and pronunciation. This is also an opportunity to talk about differences in accents, usage, spelling and so on.

UNIT 13

Drama

from Bethune

PRE-READING

Invite the class to formulate a definition of a hero and provide examples that illustrate their definition.
   Set the stage for this unit by discussing the background information on Norman Bethune.

COMPREHENSION

Questions 1, 2, 3, 6, 8 and 9 are designed to strengthen students' understanding of the text.

4. "Bastard," which refers literally to an illegitimate child, is usually an abusive term. Here, however, Bethune uses it to express his affection and respect for the bravery of the soldiers.
5. This question is designed to encourage students to think about Langley's classifications of groups.
6. "Which group(s) do you suppose the Colonel believes Bethune belongs in?" In some editions, the number is omitted.
7. These stage directions help contrast Bethune's coolness with the understandably unsteady nerves of the Colonel and Sorenson.
10. This question requires students to think about the structure of the play as consciously set up by Langley.

DISCUSSION

These questions move from a discussion of the specific characters and ideas presented in the play to broader issues on which opinions will vary.

Expand on question 5 by inviting students to give a brief oral presentation on one of the famous people listed here or on your augmented list.

VOCABULARY BUILDING

Metaphors: Visual Shorthand
Answers will vary.

Hyperbole or Exaggerated Language
Answers will vary. Here are some possibilities.

1. I could drink enough to sink a battleship.
2. That shirt is to die for!
3. X is so crooked he has to screw on his socks.
4. I'll help you when hell freezes over.
5. You call that music? A herd of cows singing opera makes better music than that!
6. X isn't playing with a full deck (of cards).
7. X is a walking encyclopedia.

WRITING

1. This assignment helps students practise composing realistic dialogue and select appropriate non-verbal cues to accompany their characters' conversation. Vary this task by dividing the class into groups and inviting each to prepare a dialogue, complete with stage directions. If the groups exchange scripts, students can act out each other's dialogues. The writers will then be able to see how clear or appropriate their non-verbal cues are.
2. This is a creative exercise in persuasive writing.
3. This character analysis is good practice for students who expect to continue in an academic program.

GRAMMAR

Verbs: Indirect Speech
Remind students to pay close attention to the tense of the verbs they use. The wording of their answers will vary.

Levels of Language

Although answers will vary, the following are some suggestions.

1. I found the film quite enjoyable and entertaining.
   Hey, that flick was cool.
2. Emily and George are exchanging vows of matrimony on Saturday.
   Emily and George are tying the knot on Saturday.
3. Hello, Raffi, would you be in a position to advance me a modest short-term loan?
   Hey Raffi, float me a few bucks till payday, will ya?
4. Have you heard the unhappy news about Lucie's dog? It seems that she has passed away.
   Guess what! Lucie's dog bought it.
5. I regret to inform you that I shall be unable to attend.
   I can't make it, okay?
6. Would you care to join me for dinner this evening?
   C'mon over for a bite to eat tonight, eh?
7. I hope you have a very pleasant afternoon (morning, etc.)
   Take care!

Editing and Proofreading: Verbs

1. Thomas suggested that I come early.
2. The quality of both George's homework assignments and his lab reports indicates his hard work.
3. Every Friday after work, Emile plays pool with his buddies.
4. James Dean made only three movies: *Rebel without a Cause*, *East of Eden* and *Giant*.
5. My car has not been working properly for the past three days.
6. When I went skiing last January, I broke my arm.
7. By the time the judges awarded the medals, they had seen each athlete perform eight times.
8. When Suzanne is 65, she will be eligible for her retirement pension.
9. If I wanted to buy a new sound system, I would study all the consumer reports for information on the best model to buy.
10. God help you if you have an accident in my brand-new car!

Part 2
Oral Activities

UNIT 14
Scenarios from Everyday Life

Each of the scenarios outlined in this unit presents a different everyday situation. Although students may not have experienced these specific predicaments themselves, most are probably similar enough to situations they have encountered that they will be able to identify with the characters.

Because two to four participants are required to role-play each scenario, the unit lends itself to groupwork. There are a number of ways to proceed; all the scenarios need not be used at once. One or even two might make a good warm-up exercise at the beginning of a class or, if the class is a long one, after a break. They might also provide a change of pace from a grammar or writing activity.

In this case, you could begin by reading the scenario(s) to the entire class, then brainstorm to come up with the vocabulary necessary to perform the roles. Give students 15 minutes or so to prepare, and five to seven minutes to present the scenario(s).

If you would like every student to participate in a single class, set aside 10 minutes or so at the end of one class to form groups and assign scenarios for the next class. Instruct students to read their own scenario, decide who is to play whom, then prepare their roles at home. You might also encourage them to meet outside class to discuss and prepare their scenario, thus extending their opportunities to practise speaking English.

Students might also videotape their scenarios as a homework activity, then present the tapes to the class. If the videos are shown over a series of classes, they can provide a welcome break from other activities.

Although this unit includes no writing activities, students could be asked to generate a composition describing one of the situations from the viewpoint of one of the participants.

UNIT 15

Short-Term Gain—Long-Term Pain?

To provide a model for organizing and working with the oral units, this unit is presented in more detail than the other selections in this section. Keep in mind, however, that it represents only one way to proceed. Depending on your own teaching style and the needs, interests and abilities of the students, many variations are possible.

PREPARATION

Begin by inviting the class to free-write for seven to 10 minutes on a topic such as, How do we balance our need for economic expansion with our need to preserve the environment? Follow this with a class discussion, asking students to cite concrete examples of situations in which economic and historical or environmental interests conflict.

READING

Read the situation on page 184 of *Reflections* with the class. Point out that this story is based on an event that actually happened in 1993. Explain that you'll tell students what really happened later on.

Discuss unfamiliar vocabulary with the class. The depth of your discussions of vocabulary, idiom, tone of voice and so on depends entirely on the needs and abilities of the students, the time available, and the emphasis you wish to place on spoken English.

ORAL ACTIVITIES

Read the list of individuals who will represent various interests in the panel discussion and debate. If the names of organizations, such as the Canadian Audubon Society, are unfamiliar to students, you can either explain them yourself or encourage students to look them up. Discuss the point of view likely to be taken by each group.

Divide the class into groups of three. Depending on your purposes, you may assign students to groups or encourage them to form their own. The students can choose their own roles on a first-come, first-served basis. You may also appoint a moderator (or a group of two or three) for the debate who can use the preparation time to draw up procedures for the discussion, deciding on time limits, setting up the order of speakers, organizing the question period and preparing to summarize the findings.

Take this opportunity to review appropriate vocabulary. For example, while it may be acceptable to use slang such as "jerk" or "bleeding heart" in a conversation with friends, these emotionally "loaded" terms are not appropriate in formal argument, because they attack the speaker rather than the argument.

Allow 15 or 20 minutes for the groups to prepare their arguments. Many teachers use this as an opportunity to observe individual students in a group conversation, making anecdotal records of their strengths and weaknesses that can be discussed later. It's also an opportunity to circulate to offer assistance; however, if students seem to be getting on well, feel free to leave them alone.

Before the panel discussion begins, either you or the student moderator needs to explain the procedures. Once the discussion is over, the moderator sums up the arguments and provides a synopsis of the debate.

Now, ask the class what they think actually happened in Winnipeg. You might put the matter to a vote.

The Answer: Such a hue and cry—petitions, letters, radio phone-in shows and so on—arose over the proposed destruction of the trees that the city council voted to refuse the Hollywood studio's offer. (Many students who argue for preserving the trees are surprised to discover that Winnipeg refused the offer. They are cynical enough to believe that big business always wins. Others believe that Winnipeg made the wrong decision.)

WRITING

Invite the class to recap the arguments for and against accepting the film studio's offer and record the points on the chalkboard. The writing activity can be assigned for homework.

UNIT 16

Inheritance

This situation represents a scenario most of us have dreamed about: unexpectedly receiving a large inheritance from an eccentric relative who placed no restrictions on how it ought to be spent.

PREPARATION

Begin by suggesting that the class free-write on a related but unspecific free-writing topic such as, If I won the lottery, I would.... This sparks students to think about what they would do with a windfall.

ORAL ACTIVITIES

Read the situation and ask students to imagine what someone working at an entry-level position with a small investment firm might be like. For instance, this person might have inherited something besides money from Aunt Hattie. Depending on the direction the conversation takes, the issue of stereotypes can be introduced.

Form the class into groups of three and assign each group one of the possibilities for disposing of the inheritance. The discussion can be extended by asking students how each plan for using the legacy reflects the personality and character of the recipient.

WRITING

This enables the students to venture into their imaginations to "invent" the colorful Aunt Hattie.

UNIT 17

Desperately Seeking...

The situation introduces a familiar phenomenon of modern life: the dating service.

PREPARATION

Invite students to free-write on a related but unspecific topic such as, The best way to meet people you might want to date is...

To prepare for the discussion questions, ask students to bring in ads for dating services or from a newspaper personal column.

ORAL ACTIVITIES

Group Discussion

These questions can be discussed either before or after reading the description of Susan Micone's love life.

The Dating Game

The discussion may raise issues that go well beyond the value of dating services. For example, some students may reject Vince Lombardi out-of-hand because he is divorced. In these discussions, it is important to strike a balance between encouraging free expression and discouraging intolerance.

WRITING

These topics require students to organize and develop ideas logically. The first two simply require an outline of the pros and cons of a specific issue; the third asks them to adopt and argue a position.

The tasks may either provide practice in a type of writing that has already been covered during the reading units, or form the basis of a lesson on how to approach an essay topic that asks students to agree or disagree.

UNIT 18

Whose Needs Come First?

Because strong arguments can be made for all the proposals, students can focus on developing their powers of logical argument.

PREPARATION

Invite the class to free-write on a topic such as, The architecture of an institution or workplace should promote high morale and encourage a sense of community rather than be purely functional.

ORAL ACTIVITIES

If necessary, create a seventh group by dividing the second proposal in two: one group can represent the interests of the disabled students and a second those of the overall student population. Students not assigned a specific proposal can function as the board, listening to the reports and deciding which is the most convincing.

WRITING

Discuss the formatting and organization of formal reports and stress the importance of strengthening arguments with specific detail.

Expand the unit to include an *authentic* writing assignment by discussing areas of your own institution that need improvement. Decide which problem is likely to receive attention—a suggestion to build a new library would probably not be taken seriously, while a proposal to install lights along the path to the parking lot might.

Encourage students to write a letter to the appropriate administrator identifying the problem and proposing solutions. It's a good idea to explain the assignment to this person ahead of time, letting him or her know the letter is coming and requesting co-operation in providing a speedy reply.

UNIT 19

Work and the Family

Students often become quite emotionally involved in the dilemma facing Emily and George. The situation highlights a number of issues that are relevant in today's society, and often sparks discussion of different cultural attitudes:

- The roles of men and women in the family; who makes decisions?
- The working mother.
- The role of the extended family, and the degree to which adult children are responsible to and for them.
- Long-distance relationships.
- Which comes first: work or family?

PREPARATION

Invite the class to free-write on or discuss a topic such as, A husband and wife should arrive at decisions jointly; however, when there is disagreement, the husband's opinion takes precedence.

ORAL ACTIVITIES

The two activities may be combined so that every student is involved in a group activity. Form the class into groups of three. Five groups can take care of activity 2 while the rest of the class brainstorms about the entire situation.

WRITING

Writing these informal letters and dialogues enables students to "get in character" to express a particular point of view. They can address the issues emotionally and express their views wholeheartedly.

UNIT 20

The Continuing Story of...

This unit draws on students' knowledge of commercial television. It invites them to create their own soap operas, while developing their awareness of the formula underlying the success of most TV dramas.

PREPARATION

Invite students to name soap operas—daytime or evening—they have watched. Discuss the reasons for the popularity of these series. As a group activity, you might ask them to discuss and compare several shows and identify characters or plot lines that are similar.

They might also free-write on a topic such as, Soap operas provide an accurate reflection of the everyday things that concern us.

ORAL ACTIVITIES

When introducing these activities, you might encourage students to create settings that are culturally familiar. For example, a group might decide to set its soap opera in the community's Chinatown or "Little Italy." This assignment could empower students to explore and articulate areas of cultural conflict through the fictional characters and situations. As a result, continuing this project over a semester, as suggested in the follow-up activity, may provide benefits beyond merely practising English skills.

WRITING

These topics help students develop analytical skills that are useful in many academic subjects. In addition, as they begin to recognize the formulas, they may become more discriminating TV viewers.

UNIT 21
A Living Will

The situation presented in this unit centres on the ethical, and sometimes legal, implications of our growing technology. For the first time in history, we have the means to decide not whether we are *able* to prolong a life, but whether we *ought* to—as the case of Sue Rodriguez, who fought for her right to die, showed us so eloquently.

PREPARATION

Suggest that the class free-write on or discuss a topic such as, Under what circumstances, if any, should an individual have the right to determine when his or her life should end?

ORAL ACTIVITIES

Because students often have strong feelings about this subject, this is an opportunity to stress the principles of debate, whereby one argues a position logically, regardless of one's personal convictions.

While part of the class is preparing the five conflicting points of view to present to the "court," the rest of the students might discuss the benefits and drawbacks of our adversarial legal system.

WRITING

These topics involve the straightforward elaboration of a clear thesis.

RESEARCH

You might combine this assignment with a tour of your institution's library. Most librarians welcome opportunities to provide a short guided tour or lecture about their facilities and resources—an excellent supplementary activity for students.

UNIT 22

Best Interests of the Child

Though many details have been changed, this story is based on an actual incident that occurred several years ago in Australia. Our shrinking world, a growing number of inter-cultural marriages and rising divorce rates have created new areas of potential conflict.

PREPARATION

Ask the class to free-write on or discuss one of the following topics:

— Inter-cultural marriages seldom work.
— In a divorce, children under 12 should automatically remain with their mother.
— In a divorce involving an inter-cultural marriage, the children should remain with the father because they need to stay in touch with their cultural heritage.

ORAL ACTIVITIES

It's a good idea to read and discuss the situation with the class before assigning these activities. It's important to present this scenario not in terms of the "rightness" of one "side," but as the story of two people who find themselves playing out a conflict caused by differences in their cultural values. Students may volunteer stories from their own experience that relate to the scenario.

Encouraging students to role-play characters they feel sympathy for may help develop some of the background issues that are implied rather than stated, especially in conversations 1 and 4.

WRITING

Each of these topics requires students to adopt a position on the Salim case, and to support their view with persuasive reasoning.

UNIT 23

The Best Candidate

This situation, requiring students to choose the best candidate for a specific job, raises a number of relevant issues, such as:

— Employment equity, including possible discrimination on the basis of age, gender, state of health and marital status;
— The value of a post-secondary education in a specific area versus on-the-job experience and a successful track record.

The ideas complement the theme of Unit 3—Going for the Gold.

PREPARATION

Invite students to free-write on or discuss a topic such as, Which is more important when applying for a job: education or experience?

ORAL ACTIVITIES

Encourage students to review the profiles with a critical eye—to read between the lines. For example, because we request letters of reference from people who are likely to say positive things about us, can a description such as "competent and reliable" (Howard Heinrich) be construed as ambiguous? Is there hidden meaning behind a statement such as, "Mr. X undoubtedly has potential"?

Invite students to bring in Help Wanted ads for jobs that sound interesting. Suggest that they role-play interviews in pairs.

WRITING

The first two topics are straightforward comparisons while the third requires the writer to be sensitive to the feelings of the reader. The fourth is a creative piece, while the fifth asks students to analyse and draw a conclusion about one aspect of North American society.

UNIT 24

Who's at Fault?

The situation presented in this unit is based on an actual incident, although some details have been added for dramatic effect.

PREPARATION

Invite the class to free-write on or discuss a topic such as, Describe a travel experience—your own or someone else's—that demonstrates how hard it is to understand another culture.

This unit is an excellent follow-up to Unit 1—A Traveller's Tale.

ORAL ACTIVITIES

Creating Dialogue

After reading and discussing Julia's experience, encourage students to dramatize the situation by role-playing the 10 suggested dialogues. These informal dialogues should explore the implications of Julia's "adventure."

On Trial

The trial enables students to develop the central aspects of the situation in a more formal way. To involve the entire class, the eight or nine active roles can be discussed and prepared in groups of three.

WRITING

Begin by asking students how they would approach these topics. Focus in particular on considering how the purpose of the piece and the target audience may affect what they say. How appropriate is it to include personal opinions or assign blame? What tone and level of vocabulary should be used? And so on.

UNIT 25

Whodunit?

Everyone loves a murder mystery. The purpose of this one is not to find the correct solution—there is none!—but to come up with a convincing theory based on the detailed evidence presented.

The story follows the Agatha Christie model: except for the detective and the staff, everyone is a suspect. The trick is to sift the evidence—revealing *how, when* and *where* the crime was committed—then come up with a motive—*why* should lead to *who*dunit!

PREPARATION

Invite the class to free-write on a topic such as, Why are murder mysteries so popular in books, TV and movies?

ORAL ACTIVITIES

While pretty much anything goes in terms of a solution, students should ensure that all the evidence is accounted for and explained. Their solution should answer the five essential questions: *how, when, where* and *why* the crime was committed—and *who*dunit.

WRITTEN ACTIVITIES

These follow the same pattern as topics suggested in previous units.

FOLLOW-UP

1. Students might enjoy making a videotape of this whodunit suitable for a half-hour TV segment.
2. Invite students to create their own murder mysteries, possibly in groups. If the class has extended the soap opera (see Unit 20) into more episodes, a murder might be integrated into the plot.